D1238019

A PHILOSOPHY OF MAN

A
Philosophy
of
Man

by
ADAM SCHAFF

A DELTA BOOK

A Delta Book

Published by Dell Publishing Co., Inc.
750 Third Avenue, New York, New York 10017
Copyright © 1963 by Adam Schaff
First published in the United States in 1963 by
Monthly Review Press

Delta ® TM 755118, Dell Publishing Co., Inc.
By arrangement with Lawrence & Wishart Ltd.,
London, England
Printed in U.S.A.
Second Printing

This book is translated from the Polish,
and the translation has been revised throughout
by the author for English publication.
The verses of Heine, quoted in Chapter 14,
are translated by Jack Lindsay.

FOREWORD

This book is made up of a collection of essays written at different times. In making them available to the English reader I would like to explain their origin and the guiding thought behind their combination into one volume.

The political and moral shocks of 1955—57 created in Poland a growth of interest in the problems of the individual, especially amongst the younger intellectuals. And from this ensued a rapid growth of the influence of Existentialism, since it was the only philosophy which seemed to concentrate on answering the questions raised. To oppose this tendency became for Marxists, therefore, not only a theoretical but a political necessity. And this demanded not only a reasoned and convincing philosophical criticism of Existentialism but a positive treatment from the Marxist standpoint of the same problems. We had to oppose our own answers to the Existentialist answers. For the most effective criticism of alien ideology is always positive--not limiting oneself to saying "no", but proposing better solutions of the problems.

Such was the origin of these essays. They were all conceived as parts of a single argument which would both oppose Existentialism and attempt a positive solution of the problems raised.

The first part of the argument, which I have headed "Marxism and Existentialism", tries to show why Marxists must reject the Existentialist solution of the problems of the individual, but not the problems themselves. The subject matter of Existentialism has a practical importance, as our experiences in the last few years have

demonstrated. The fact that a philosophy which for various reasons we reject is engaged with these problems does not mean that they are not real problems. Nor does it mean that we necessarily reject every partial solution offered by an alien philosophy. This applies particularly to the capital discovery by Existentialism of the existence of conflicting moral situations, a discovery which delivered a death blow to the idea of an absolute morality and to the oversimplified moralising connected with it. And it applies to the sphere of politics as well.

The second part, "A Philosophy of Man", indicates the direction in which a true solution of the problems may be sought. This includes the semantic analysis of the questions presented, which at least serves to make them more precise and to isolate those for which in general there are no answers, because the questions are badly posed.

The third part, "Conflicting Humanisms", goes on to treat the problems of the individual in relation to social conditions. The solutions of problems of individual freedom and happiness proposed by various types of contemporary humanism are discussed. The variety of these approaches generates conflicts which lie at the root of much of the ideological controversy of our time.

These essays are, deliberately, not "erudite". Indeed, in certain situations erudition is a mere external embellishment which does not help but hinders. This is not a "learned" book. Worse, the answers are incomplete. And this is so because none of the problems raised are capable of complete and final solution. It is also due to the fact that we are operating on ground still largely unexplored by Marxist thought. But after all, such a provisional exploration is perhaps the best way to stimulate discussion. We must begin to think more broadly and deeply about the Marxist standpoint on these problems.

ADAM SCHAFF
Warsaw, 1962

CONTENTS

PART ONE.   MARXISM AND EXISTENTIALISM

PART TWO.   A PHILOSOPHY OF MAN

PART THREE.   CONFLICTING HUMANISMS

PART ONE

MARXISM AND EXISTENTIALISM

I

THE POPULAR APPEAL
OF EXISTENTIALISM

The sudden eruption of Existentialist influence is one of the most interesting phenomena in the intellectual life of Poland in recent years. It is interesting not only from a philosophical but also—and perhaps primarily—from a sociological and psychological point of view. Existentialism had previously been ignored in our country and was foreign to our traditions. At any rate, when in 1951 we began an offensive against non-Marxist trends in our philosophy, Existentialism was entirely left out of our plan. And yet a few years later, in 1956—57, it became a real force—especially in Marxist circles, where all kinds of so-called original and innovating ideas were simply borrowed from the Existentialists. The deep ignorance of Existentialism in both Marxist and Positivist circles contributed to this illusion of newness and originality. Even among Catholic groups there was a sudden revival of varieties of Existentialism. The sudden and tremendous appeal exerted by Existentialist ideas in an environment previously unfavourable requires primarily a sociological analysis—but not exclusively; it has also its strictly philosophical aspect.

Much recent philosophical controversy in Poland has had a hopeless appearance, as though the two sides were trying to cross swords without ever coming into direct contact. For two quite different conceptions of philosophy were represented. One side maintained that philosophy is the science of the most general laws governing all reality, while the other saw in it primarily the contemplation of human life, in the sense of the individual's proper behaviour towards himself and others, without ever demanding of such contemplation the highly exacting methods of science. This difference, however, did not take the form only of a disagreement as to what philosophy is and what its tasks are; it also showed itself, indirectly, in the treatment of various particular problems posed on the basis of different conceptions of philosophy.

This division of viewpoints on philosophy is not only of contemporary importance but is sanctified by long tradition, though we can by no means regard the division as exhaustive. Let us recall, for example, the queer though in its time influential view (rejected today even by its authors) that philosophy is the logical analysis of scientific propositions. This was one of the many ephemeral phenomena in the history of philosophy, whereas the viewpoints we have indicated rest on a long history which, among other things, attests to their vitality. Both reach back to ancient Greece—the one to the Ionian philosophy, which set out to discover "the substance" of the world and how, from one substance, all the multifarious phenomena of nature and of human life could arise; and the other to the Socratic school, which set such matters on one side and concentrated on the practical and moral problems of human existence. It is in this sense that we may speak of the Ionian and Socratic traditions in the history of philosophy.

The harking back of today's antagonists to those remote and valued traditions is well based. In the Ionian tradition, although the original speculations combined spontaneous reflections of reality with religious myths, there exist the germs of all modern tendencies to link philosophy with science and to see its specific domain as the investigation of the most general laws governing the world. (What is understood here by "world", and how the relation of philosophy to particular sciences is understood, are questions on which there arises a divergence of views within the framework of the broad conception of the task of philosophy.) According to Cicero, Socrates was the philosopher who brought philosophy down from heaven to earth and directed it to the human hearth.

Alongside the fundamental division of philosophies into materialist and idealist it is possible to apply various other divisions: for example, empiricism and rationalism, rationalism and irrationalism, static and dynamic views and so on. All these divisions are connected in one way or another, but not always in the sense of their uniform disposition along the lines of the central division into materialism and idealism. That is why the history of philosophy can by no means be depicted all in "black and white". It is by no means the case historically that materialism was always right in everything and idealism always wrong. This applies particularly to the issues of the conflict between the Ionian and Socratic traditions. That conflict is certainly connected with the division between materialism and idealism—but to point that out does not resolve the controversy. For materialism, like idealism, can include various conceptions of the subject matter of philosophy and various solutions of the conflict between Ionian and Socratic traditions. Moreover, like other divisions, this division has not been historically "pure". Only in extreme cases have the adherents of the broad Ionian tradition rejected all interest in questions of morality. Similarly, the advocates of the Socratic conception of philosophy have seldom divorced themselves entirely from ontological problems connected with the theory of perception. This is attested by the example of even such extremist trends as Neo-Positivism and Existentialism in the contemporary world.

And there is a simple explanation for this. It confirms

the truth that real theoretical problems cannot be dismissed merely by denying that they exist. To do so can have only one result, namely, that someone else will deal with those problems and win a reputation by so doing. To try to "conceal America" is an idea worthy of Gogol's hero. To discover America—supposing that something is really there to be discovered—means that America can no longer be concealed, regardless of whether the discoverer has a true or false conception of what he has discovered. Thus regardless of our views on the subject matter of philosophy and on its range of interests, and as to whether the questions dealt with by the Socratic approach to philosophy are allowable or not, no-one is able to "conceal" those questions. And this is so, simply because they are living questions with which every person, in one way or another, sooner or later, is confronted.

It is possible, of course, to deny the reality of the questions and so eliminate the need for answers. But that is merely a typical case of "concealing America". Neo-Positivism, with its doctrine of so-called "pseudo-problems", may serve as a classical example. This doctrine purports to demonstrate, among other things, that statements of morality, while having the grammatical form of sentences, are without any definite meaning. Do the Neo-Positivists wish to say the same about many of the problems discussed by Existentialists—for instance, the problem of "the meaning of life and death"? No doubt they would argue, and rightly, that the question: "What is the meaning of life?" cannot be answered in the same way as, say, the question: "What is the temperature of a fluid?". But it does not follow from this that the problem disappears, or is not a philosophical problem. In fact, while the Neo-Positivists continue to talk about "pseudo-problems", those same "pseudo-problems" are making a philosophical career for themselves. This is not at all because the problems have been mystified, although their partial mystification by the Existentialists has played a big role in their dissemination among the masses. It is because they arise, whatever the Neo-Positivists may say, from the realities of human existence and from real human needs.

Unfortunately it is not only Neo-Positivists who have been guilty of dismissing these questions. Sins in this respect were also committed—though in a different way, for different reasons, and on the basis of opposite principles—by Marxists. And this fact has played its part in the development of the ideological struggle among us in Poland.

Marxism, unlike Neo-Positivism, presents no doctrinal obstacles to entertaining the problems about the role and place of the individual which have lately, among us, been monopolised by Existentialism. On the contrary, Marxism originated, in great measure, from precisely this field of interest, although from the start Marx posed the problems in a way contrary to that adopted by the Existentialists. For example, the whole concept of "alienation" in Marx's early writings belongs to this field. Nevertheless, these problems were not only neglected in the further development of Marxism, but came to be regarded by some Marxists as alien and hostile, because opponents had magnified them from a false, idealist standpoint. But in this way the Marxists played into the hands of those others, especially the Existentialists—allowing them to claim a monopoly in socially important problems and thereby create the false impression that such problems could be resolved only by an idealist, subjectivist approach.

Why did this happen? Why did so many Marxists first neglect these problems and then withdraw from them? It was primarily because the union of Marxism with the revolutionary working-class movement demanded concentration on the laws of social development, the laws of the transition to socialism and of the construction of socialism, and problems connected with the immediate struggles of the masses. These practical, political interests of Marxism tended to push aside questions connected with the individual and his specific problems, to future consideration. And later, after the victory of the proletariat, when the conditions for entertaining these questions were objectively much more favourable, other obstacles intervened which exerted an ever greater counter-force. The enemies of Marxism seized upon these problems and fashioned them into ideological weapons against the revolutionary working-class movement. The odium of the struggle was transferred to these problems which were being used by enemy forces who had made of them something alien and hostile. This was, of course, a mistaken reaction—but psychologically understandable.

The fact that many Polish Marxists not only failed to reckon with these problems but treated them as enemy territory created a deficiency in our philosophical arsenal. Sartre correctly called attention to this deficiency in his article "Marxism and Existentialism" in the Polish journal *Twórczość* (1957, p 4). And that at the present time this cannot be regarded as an unimportant deficiency is demonstrated by the fact that the Revisionist tendency in our country has borrowed heavily from Existentialism and has in fact been sailing under its flag.

Without fear of vulgar sociologising, it is possible to explain the origin and continued influence of Existentialism in Europe in the 19th and 20th centuries by reference to social factors. There is an evident connection between the Existentialist way of thinking and the moral and political crises and social shocks which occur in a period of the rise of a new social formation and the fall of an old one. They generate on the one hand interest in the laws of social development and studies in this field, while inducing, on the other hand, concern about the individual and his fate. True, problems about the individual are always with us—the problem of death and of the meaning of life, for example. But there are times when this kind of problem is presented in the most urgent way by life itself. This occurs when there is general loss of confidence in the stability of the social order, when social conflicts produce moral and political crises, and when people are presented with choices in a situation where the established traditional criteria no longer exist. This explains, among other things, the mass appeal of Existentialism in many European countries after the second world war. Many people saw in its theme the reflection of their own concern; and the Existentialist atmosphere of mental depression, the sense of resignation, the sense of the helplessness of the individual grappling with omnipotent and irrational forces, reflected their own sentiments.

These factors acted all the more forcefully under the specific conditions in Poland after 1956. Here we had not only a general undermining of criteria of judgment, not only a widespread crisis of values and a feeling of the insecurity of one's fate and of the senselessness of conscious activity, the usual accompaniments of stormy periods of wars and revolutions. There arose in our country, at least among certain circles, an even fiercer storm. The disclosure by the international Communist movement of what we call in our jargon "mistakes and distortions" was for many a moral and political earthquake, which induced moral crises varying in form and degree. Normally, the crisis was all the deeper, among those who lived through it, the brighter their horizons had been, the more pronounced their previous attitude of blind faith, and the smaller their knowledge of reality. This has to be understood as a real and deep process, regardless of the scum of animosity, snobbism and ordinary careerism which it brought to the surface. We must not allow the scum to obscure for us the deep currents underneath. Without investigating and understanding the nature of these currents among us we cannot undertake remedial action, particularly in the field of ideology.

Is there anything strange in the fact that those who formerly submitted blindly to all orders because they believed in their correctness should, in the face of the revealed abuses, now raise questions about the individual's responsibility for his actions and the conflict between conscience and discipline? Is it surprising that such people should raise questions about the role of the individual in the mass movement, and about how he is to decide for himself in the case of conflicts between what he is called upon to do and his own standards of right and wrong? No, whoever has undergone such an experience and not raised such questions is either a complete primitive or suffers from the worst kind of moral insensibility. These questions were not only proper, but had to be raised.

Is it surprising, then, that people turned to sources where they could find some sort of analysis of the problems perplexing them, some kind of answers to the questions oppressing them? No, it is sad that they turned to Existentialism, with its negative outlook, but fully understandable if we consider the sharp moral shocks and political disorientation they were suffering. The theoretical gap in the development of Marxist philosophy, to which I have already referred and of which Sartre speaks, had painful results with us in Poland. Those who are absent always lose the battle, and we reported absent on an important sector of the ideological front and at a rather critical moment. This is a much more serious matter than the often repeated "inadequate development of a Marxist ethics".

Only one conclusion can be drawn from all this. We must take our place in the arena as soon as possible. We must fill the existing gap by working out our standpoint on the neglected problems.

2

TOWARDS THE EFFECTIVE CRITICISM
OF NON-MARXIST IDEOLOGY

Let us begin with the following question which arises in connection with defining our attitude to the problems posed by Existentialism. Is it "academic objectivism" to admit that a philosophy criticised by us contains real problems for analysis? Our answer is: not only is there no deviation here from principled criticism but, on the contrary, this is the only effective method of criticism.

And yet the procedure within our movement in Poland has been the opposite for many years. For many years, with us, the criticism of alien ideology had a nihilistic character. In the first place, to describe any doctrine as bourgeois or idealist was taken as actually settling the matter. If analysis went any deeper into the actual content of the doctrine, that was only to dig out examples to illustrate the already accomplished general estimation — an easy thing to do, of course. Any positive elements within the given doctrine, any true or even partially true solutions of any particular questions, were simply ignored, since they did not fit into the general estimation, or were written off as "inconsequential" or "incidental".

This style of criticism became a law unto itself after Zhdanov's well known intervention in the Soviet discussion on philosophy in 1947 against "academic objectivism", which was supposed to consist primarily of finding positive elements in criticised viewpoints. After that, no-one was expected to sin against the rules of "principled criticism". As often happens in such cases, practice began rapidly to outpace the theoretical postulates. There began to flourish among us criticism in cavalier fashion, bereft of any actual citations of the opponent's views ("platforms for the enemy"), and consequently never settling accounts with him. This was aided by the practice of vulgar sociologising, which without any analysis in detail labelled the criticised viewpoints as "bourgeois" or "idealist". What a paradise it was for facile critics, whose acquaintance with the views they were criticising was too often limited to second- or even third-hand quotations!

I refer to these practices here only because of the harm they did to the struggle against bourgeois ideology, and the need for rapidly overcoming them in the interests of that struggle.

Nihilistic criticism may impress people who are already convinced, but never those who are themselves impressed by the views criticised. And yet, it is the latter we are primarily concerned with. What is more, we are made to look like fools and ignoramuses, who criticise views which we have not troubled to study, misrepresent them, and are incapable of understanding the problems they raise. With idealist views so widespread among intellectuals, such criticism has had very sad results for us. Effective criticism, on the other hand, must fulfil at least the three following basic conditions:

1) It must be based on proper knowledge and citation of the opponent's views, which must be opposed with pertinent counter-arguments.

2) It must single out in the views criticised the problems which account for their attraction, and which remain even when it is agreed that the solutions offered for them are false.

3) It must put forward alternative, positive solutions

of those problems. Criticism is effective when it not only shakes the confidence of those it addresses in the correctness of their views, but also demonstrates the superiority of the counter-solutions it proposes. If this is not done, we lose the fight from the outset. We only strengthen the resistance of those who regard the given problems as important, and often create an emotional block — the worst enemy of common sense and rational discussion.

However, the harmfulness of nihilistic criticism lies not only in its ineffectiveness, in its missing the target—which is to convince our opponents and those who are undecided. It is also harmful to ourselves, since it impoverishes our ideas and hampers their development.

One of the results of nihilistic criticism and vulgar sociologising is the dogmatic assumption that a false system can contain no real problems for analysis and much less any new, positive solution of such problems. An ostrich-like policy of believing that a problem disappears if we close our eyes to it is, of course, harmless to the opponent. But it is harmful to those who close their eyes. The consequence of ignoring problems because they are raised by ideological opponents is to eliminate them from one's own theoretical equipment and to close the door on one's own development of them.

Two concrete cases may be cited by way of example. We have criticised the semantic philosophy—and rightly—as subjectivist. But this subjectivist philosophy has nevertheless posed the important question of the active role of language in the process cognition. Who, then, would suffer if all the themes of that philosophy were placed under a taboo because its foundations are false? Only we, of course. And we must now make up for our long neglect of semantic analysis in logic, philosophy and sociology. The situation is similar with mathematical logic, cybernetics, field sociological investigation, and the problems of the individual posed by Existentialism. The claim that current theories in each of the above cases were based on false philosophical foundations was well grounded. But those who understood "principled criticism" as a negation of all the problems posed by those theories made a terrible mistake which only held up and impoverished the development of our own theory.

The Marxist system is an "open" one by its very nature. It is founded on the necessity of continually revising particular conclusions in the light of new facts and discoveries, of the continual creative development of its own theories. Marxism is always prepared to absorb new data, new discoveries, new achievements of theoretical thought, to generalise from them and, in case of need, to modify its existing propositions in the light of these generalisations. It is in this spirit that Engels spoke in his own name, and in that of his great friend, when he said that their theory was not a dogma but a guide to action, a methodology. This is why the dogmatic distortion of Marxism must be regarded, in the strict sense, as revisionism, and the worst sort of revisionism at that, because its revision of the fundamental thesis of the creative character of Marxism denies the scientific character of Marxism.

Involved here are not only theoretical but also practical considerations. The further development of Marxism must assimilate all the accomplishments of social practice, the growth of science, and so on. It is necessary to say clearly that social practice comprises also the practice of the development of science. Perhaps there is no-one who any longer doubts that the development of our theory not only may but must embrace the new theoretical acquisitions of Einstein, Planck, Bohr and others. But does this apply only to them? Are branches of knowledge of a distinct class character automatically to be excluded? Of course, the latter present a more delicate problem. The approach to them must be different. But who has the right to assert, a priori, that no real problem and no positive solution of any question can exist outside of Marxism? Practice says something else. Such an idea does not flow from any creative understanding of Marxism, but from its dogmatic distortion. This kind of understanding of the relation of Marxism to other currents of thought can have only one result—the impoverishment of Marxist thought and the consequent weakening of its influence over the masses.

Noisy nihilistic criticism is not evidence of strength but of weakness. It results from fear of open battle, whereas the ideological struggle can be won only in open battle, by convincing people with pertinent arguments.

3

THE PROBLEM OF THE INDIVIDUAL

In a debate between such contrary philosophies as
Marxism and Existentialism—I refer throughout to
Sartre's variant which has played so big a role in Poland—
it is necessary to go straight to the main point of their
differences. This concerns the concept of the individual,
which is the central concept of every variety of Existentialism, and around which are grouped all differences of
viewpoint between Existentialism and Marxism.

Does the individual create society, by choosing the
manner of his behaviour in complete spontaneity and
freedom of choice? Or is it society that creates the individual and determines his mode of behaviour?—These
questions lie at the heart of the antagonism between
Existentialism and Marxism. All others, including the
problem of "essence and existence", are consequent upon
the way they are answered.

Of course, the different points of departure by no
means signify that Existentialism completely rejects the
role of society, or Marxism that of the individual. But all
varieties of Existentialism—which differ greatly in the
areas separating Kirkegaard from Sartre—are united not
only by the fact that their central problems concern the fate
and experiences of the individual, but also by—and, indeed,
primarily by—their conception of the individual as isolated,
lonely and tragic in his senseless struggle with the alien
forces of the world around him. Involved here are problems hard to grasp and even harder to express clearly.

This standpoint is ordinarily called subjectivism; and that it actually is, despite the Existentialists' protest against such a designation of their position. Only by taking off from the position of subjectivism can one arrive at such a strange and internally contradictory conception as that of the "sovereign" individual, completely free to make decisions which depend only on himself, who is at the same time defenceless and tragic in his hopeless struggle with malicious fate. The internal contradiction that appears here is that between a voluntarist variety of subjectivism and the concept of an objective fate, independent of human activity.

Sartre's reputation is due to his skillful treatment of the central problem of all varieties of Existentialism, the problem of the individual and his complex relations with the world surrounding him. Sartre's has become the most typical variety of Existentialism. This is due not only to the atmosphere of helplessness and despair with which his whole philosophy is permeated, but to the concept which generates this atmosphere—the a-social concept of the individual who, being isolated and lonely, must determine his behaviour entirely for himself and, with nothing but his own judgment to guide him, grapple with hostile living and non-living forces. This is not a new idea, but it exerts a strong appeal in the conditions of moral chaos of the post-war world, in the conditions of the break up of traditional systems of values while new social values take shape amid conflict and pain. Its appeal is all the greater when expressed by a great writer who is at the same time an excellent psychologist.

But this is only one Sartre. There is another who, in spite of the first, leans towards socialism in his practical activities and towards Marxism in his theoretical work. There is something droll in the fact that Sartre—the Existentialist moving towards Marxism—could in an article specially written for a Polish journal teach something to our Marxists who, moving towards Existentialism, had lost their knowledge of Marxist philosophy and its values. Sartre reminded them that Marxism is the only modern philosophy which has the perspective of further development. I said that there is something amusing in this—but it is at the same time perfectly understandable. When two contrary tendencies—one away from and the other towards Marxism—intersect at a certain point, they by no means come to an agreement there. They are moving in opposite directions, and cannot agree. This is why an Existentialist moving towards Marxism understands Marxism much better than a Marxist who is moving towards Existentialism.

While fully recognising Sartre's stature and talents one should not lose sight of the inner contradictions of his views, which do not decrease but rather increase with the development of his views. There is a contradiction between the Sartre who clings to traditional Existentialism and the Sartre who pays tribute to the philosophy of Marxism. This contradiction can be overcome only by abandoning one or other of the two antagonistic views he now holds. And it is concentrated mainly in his conception of the individual.

The young Marx, whom certain of his "admirers" in Poland wish violently to transform into an Existentialist, wrote in his famous *Theses on Feuerbach*: "The human essence is no abstraction inherent in each single individual. In its reality it is the ensemble of the social relations." This statement, aphoristic in form, was directed against Feuerbach, who in Marx's opinion did not understand the social individual and so comitted a double sin: (1) against the *historical* conditioning of the individual, whom Feuerbach conceived abstractly as an isolated being; (2) against his *social* conditioning, which Feuerbach conceived in a naturalistic way in terms of the bonds uniting the individual members of a species.

Referring to Feuerbach's views on the individual's religious beliefs, Marx further wrote: "Feuerbach consequently does not see that the 'religious sentiment' is itself a social product, and that the abstract individual whom he analyses belongs in reality to a particular form of society."

It requires no special keeness of mind to realise that what Marx said hits not only at Feuerbach but strikes with equal force at the mistaken approach to the individual of both modern naturalism and Existentialism.

Marx states that "the human essence is no abstraction inherent in each individual. In its reality it is the ensemble of the social relations." This statement goes to the heart of the problem—if we discount the fact that this would not be today the ordinary way of phrasing this thought. The human being, as an individual, is "the ensemble of the social relations", in the sense that his origin and development can be understood only in the social and historical context, in the sense that he is the *product* of social life. This social and therefore historical approach to the investigation of the spiritual life of man and his works is the indisputable and tremendously important theoretical content of Marxism, freeing it from the limitations of both naturalism and Existentialist subjectivism in the analysis of human affairs.

It is important to emphasise this point not only in opposition to Existentialism but also to the vulgarised interpretation of the position held by the young Marx. I have already referred to the causes which led our latest revisionists to plagiarise Existentialism. The same causes led indirectly to the distortion and Existentialist vulgarisation of the young Marx. The great enthusiasm of some of our intellectuals for the themes treated by the young Marx—and this is, moreover, a broader phenomenon of international significance—can be explained by their quest for answers to their pervasive question about human affairs, their desire to "humanise the problems posed by Marxist theory, to saturate these problems with a humanist content, to connect them with the fate of the individual. That theme and its inspiration are, of course, comprised in the works of the young Marx. It is important to deepen one's analysis of this theme, making use of the further development of Marx's thought. But that is a task by no means connected only with the immediate social stimuli which actually propelled the theme to the fore.

The very social causes and spiritual shocks which caused the defection of some intellectuals, formerly connected with Marxism, to Existentialism led to their misrepresenting the tenets of the young Marx in the spirit of Existentialism. When, in contradiction with historical facts, they vulgarised their interpretation of the views of the young Marx, it was by no means with them a question of an objective investigation. It is in this light that one may understand the ignorant attempts, made with such boastfulness and aplomb by our revisionists, to counterpose the young Marx not only to Engels but also to the older Marx. For such enthusiasts, Marx was finished somewhere around 1846.

And yet it is precisely in the teachings of the young Marx that we find a firm and decisive refutation of Existentialist views on the problems of the individual. The views expressed by Marx on these problems, already expounded in the *Theses on Feuerbach*, and developed in his later theoretical works, constitute a rejection of the theoretical foundations of Existentialism—subjectivism, the a-social and a-historical conception of the individual.

The internal contradictions of Sartre's views are related precisely to this question. It is not possible simultaneously to pay tribute to the tenets of both Existentialism and Marxism on philosophical problems in general and the problem of the individual in particular, without falling into eclecticism and toleration of contradictions. If one approaches the problem of the individual in a Marxist way, that is, historically and socially, one must abandon the idealist, subjectivist foundations of Existentialism.

One must reject the thesis that because the individual must make independent decisions in situations of moral conflict—true, a real problem is involved here—he is condemned to loneliness and consequently to helplessness and despair. On the contrary, Marxism shows that the individual, in making independent decisions and, in a certain sense, choosing between given attitudes and activities, always does so socially, in the sense of the social conditioning of his personality. Marxism teaches that the individual's attitudes are social products, and that, in adopting the attitudes he does, the individual "belongs in reality to a particular form of society". In this light, the "philosophy of despair" has its basis only in the attitudes of certain social classes who lose their so-called "eternal" philosophical truths at turning points of history. There is a fundamental contradiction between Marxism and Existentialism. It is possible to choose between these two alternative points of view; what is not possible is to combine them into one consistent system of thought.

We may note here that even atheistic Existentialism is much closer to the tenets of religion on the problems of the obligations and destiny of individuals than would appear at first sight. This is the price of departing from the social and historical analysis of human affairs.

I have already pointed out that Existentialism contains a contradiction between the postulate of the "sovereignty" of the individual, who is supposedly the independent creator of his own destiny (in the deepest sense, this is the thesis that "existence" is prior to "essence"), and the whole content of the "philosophy of despair". For that philosophy proclaims that man is a mere pawn in the hands of fate. As Sartre indicates primarily in his plays, evil triumphs regardless of human choosing (this conception perhaps finds its sharpest expression in Sartre's play *The Devil and the Good God*). But this is precisely the antinomy of religious moralists, especially those who derive their morality from the Mosaic religion, of which Christianity is a copy. The Judaic Jehovah and the Existentialist Fate are the one as spiteful as the other: they truly create man "in their own image". They give him, cunningly enough, the power to recognise good and evil, but only so that they may condemn him. This miserable worm, with such means of knowledge at his command as the Ten Commandments, racks his brains as to what to do in life's conflicting situations and lives in a state of discord and fear, only to earn condemnation at the end. And yet this miserable and helpless creature, worthy of both pity and contempt, is in the light of religion the sovereign individual, God's highest creation! Atheistic and religious Existentialism alike repeat the tale of the cruelty and maliciousness of the old Jehovah. They create their individual as supposedly sovereign in order to make him lonely. They condemn to helplessness and despair the wretched puppets who are the sport of malicious fate while wearing the hollow crown of "sovereignty". For it is clear that the separation of the individual from society does not give him any sovereignty. On the contrary, it deprives him of all real independence. This cannot be doubted if one reads Kafka's *Trial* and *The Castle*, or sees on the stage the fate of Sartre's hero in *The Devil and the Good God*. The "philosophy of despair" is humanism inside-out; it is in essence amoral morality, dehumanised humanism.

But enough of that. What most concerns us here is that it is actually possible to choose between Marxism and Existentialism, but impossible to combine them into one. Sartre himself will, sooner or later, have to make such a choice. It is impossible to complement Marxism with Existentialism. This does not mean, however, that to be a Marxist one must give up the *subject matter* of Existentialism.

In his article on *Marxism and Existentialism* Sartre

stated that his Existentialism only fills in the gap which now exists in Marxism, and that the moment this is accomplished Existentialism loses all reason for existence as an independent current of thought.

It all depends on how the above statement is to be understood. If it is a matter of "completing" Marxism with the theory and methodology of Existentialism, then Sartre's proposition is very doubtful, since fire cannot complete water. But if it is a matter of Marxism undertaking, on the basis of the Marxist method, a more thorough investigation of the problems of the individual, which it has tended to neglect and which have been monopolised by Existentialism, then we have here an important proposal.

If it is true that Existentialism has raised questions which profoundly affect people and we have neglected them, and if it is true that this neglect has had political consequences, then it becomes important to get clear, in the first place, about exactly what questions are involved.

The usual answer is: Marxism has neglected the problems of ethics, and so it is necessary to undertake a comprehensive study of the broad principles of morality. This is true; but it is a truth of the kind that says little. What exactly is the object of a comprehensive study of the principles of morality, and how is it to be done? When it comes to the point, little remains for such studies but fine phrases.

A serious analysis of what amongst the problems posed by Existentialism is of most concern to people today brings two complexes of problems to the fore:

1) the problems of personal responsibility for one's actions, including political action and particularly in situations involving conflicts between opposing moral standards;

2) the problems of the individual's place and role in the world, which have been rather hazily expressed as "the problem of the meaning of life".

These are not single problems, but complexes of problems. They belong to the sphere of the science of morality, broadly conceived; but unhappily they were not in evidence when the traditional themes of Marxist ethics were developed. Because of that, the demand for the general "development of Marxist ethics" cannot be considered satisfactory. For the whole difficulty lies precisely in the question of how the subject is to be understood, i. e. what is the range of the problems of this ethics. By picking on particular problems we shall not, of course, develop a whole theory of ethics; but we may at least say something definite.

When an Existentialist raises problems of the individual's responsibility he does so in a rhetorical and abstract manner. And this he cannot help. For by removing the problem of the freedom of choice and responsibility of the individual from its social and historical context he cannot but treat the individual and his responsibility as abstractions. Sartre understands very well the conflicting character of situations in real life which present the individual with a choice as to how he will behave —he has expressed this in his work *L'Existentialisme est un Humanisme*, and in his literary works; but he considers this choice as the free act of the individual. We cannot accept this abstract way of posing the problem of the individual's responsibility.

How has this problem actually presented itself to us, arising from recent experiences? The problem of responsibility for one's deeds did not present itself to us in a purely theoretical and abstract form, but in a most living and practical way in conflict between party discipline and one's conscience, and in judgment of those who, not motivated by any personal considerations, were guilty of evil deeds under the conviction that they were fulfilling their social obligations.

Existentialism cannot answer problems posed in this concrete way. Its abstract and subjectivist outlook is useless in relation to such problems. To deal with them requires the development of a whole complex of theories, and first of all the sociological theory of *the individual in society* and, connected with this, the dialectics of personal freedom and the necessities flowing from social determinism. Here we find already a firm theoretical foundation in Marxism. But there arise also a number of more neglected question, of which the chief is that of the definition of responsibility in its sociological, psychological and moral aspects. Finally, there arises the difficult problem of conflicting situations and the definition of responsibility in relation to them.

Standard theories of ethics tend to overlook the fact that in real life moral judgments often relate to conflicting situations. So standard ethics simplifies its tasks and promulgates *absolute* solutions of moral problems independently of time, place and social circumstances. All religious systems and most so-called lay codes of morals attempt to do this.

All absolute ethical systems, so called, erected on the basis of supposedly eternal and immutable moral truths, are helpless before the problems occurring most often in life, namely, situations of conflict in which doing what is thought to be right brings about evil consequences. Uncertainty here does not arise because the so-called sinner is ignorant of the moral norm obligatory for him in the given situation; the moralist may come forward with his pompous commandments and prohibitions, but that does not help, because the situation is connected with a clash of contradictory standards and the poor sinner cannot decide which has priority. This may be called an "Orestes" situation. Such situations confound all "absolute" moral systems, religious or lay. Existentialism has the merit of having been aware of the problem, although it cannot solve it. Marxism has the best equipment for solving it, but has so far remained somewhat aloof.

The second main complex of problems relates to questions which are only reluctantly mentioned by philosophies pretending to the name of science. These problems, it is said, are so hazy and so burdened with tradition, that they should be regarded as belonging to the spheres of religion, mysticism or poetry rather than science. Such, indeed, is the opinion of the Neo-Positivists, who class them among "pseudo-problems". But as I have already pointed out, to call a problem a "pseudo-problem" does not abolish it; it merely hands the problem over to those least equipped to tackle it seriously. The traditional mystification of a problem does not abolish either the problem or the possibility of its scientific analysis. "What is the meaning of life?" "What is man's place in the universe?" It seems difficult to express oneself scientifically on such hazy topics. And yet if one should assert ten times over that these are typical pseudo-problems, problems would remain. Let us therefore consider what is behind the haze.

"Vanity, vanity, all is vanity!" These words, repeated in various forms in all philosophies of the East, seem to appeal to many who in old age begin to reflect on life and death. It is possible to shrug this off with a compassionate smile as nonsense. And yet the words echo a problem which cannot simply be ignored. Nor can the questions "Why?" "What for?" which force their way to the lips of people tired of the adversities and delusions of life. This applies all the more to the compulsive questions which come from reflection on death—why all this effort to stay alive if we are going to die anyway? It is difficult to evade the feeling that death is senseless—avoidable, accidental death especially. Of course, we can ask: senseless from what point of view? From the point of view of the progression of nature death is entirely sensible. But from the point of view of a given individual, death is senseless and places in doubt everything he does. Religion has tried to counter this feeling of senselessness.

The old and very wise religions of the East pointed to *nirvana* as the final goal, thus giving death a clear meaning. Other, more primitive, religions instil faith in a life after death. But what is to be done when religious belief itself loses all sense?

Attempts to ridicule all this do not help at all. The fact alone of some agnostics undergoing deathbed conversions gives much food for thought. Philosophy must take the place of religion here. It must tackle a number of diverse questions which have remained from the wreck of the religious view of life—the senselessness of suffering, of broken lives, of death, and many, many other questions relating to the fate of living, struggling, suffering and dying individuals. Can this be done scientifically, that is, in a way that is communicable and subject to some form of verification? It certainly can. True, not by following the same methods as in physics or chemistry—for this is not a matter of physics or chemistry. This is why the Neo-Positivists are wrong in their sweeping verdict that these are empty pseudo-problems. And so are those Marxists who fail just as dismally to express themselves on these question, and who cover their scornful silence by concentrating attention exclusively on great social processes and their laws of development. These are undoubtedly very important and socially decisive matters. But they do not provide automatic solutions to problems relating to individuals.

4

EXISTENTIALISED MARXISM

Sartre's latest work, *Critique of Dialectical Reason*, covers 755 pages and is only the first volume of what promises to be a monumental treatise. It must regretfully be stated that if Sartre were identified only with this strictly philosophical work he would remain an obscure and relatively unimportant philosopher. What Sartre writes as a philosopher is terribly muddled and communicates little. Although he is a Frenchman, Sartre has managed to embody in his writings the worst traditions of German pedantry and obscurity. His pages resemble, not Descartes or Diderot, but Husserl and Heidegger. Luckily, there is another Sartre, who wields a different pen and contrives as a dramatist to make clear "what the author wished to say". Thus Sartre the dramatist and novelist formerly clarified and popularised the philosophy of *L'Etre et le Néant*. Perhaps he will do the same later for his new book—though it is hard to conceive how he will do it.

Let us leave aside, however, the question of the lucidity of Sartre's new book—few philosophers are lucid anyway—and apply ourselves to its contents. The wealth of problems posed compels selection. We are interested here primarily in those which bear on Sartre's relations to Marxism and exhibit the internal contradictions of his standpoint.

Sartre has travelled far from *L'Etre et le Néant* to *Critique de la Raison Dialectique*. He of course continues on the line of Existentialist thought, but arrives at the conclusion—surprising for his creed— that Marxism is actually the great philosophy of our time. In the Introduction he writes:

> "I consider Marxism to be the undated philosophy of our time... while the ideology of Existentialism and its method of cognition is an enclave of Marxism itself, which simultaneously gives birth to it and denies it."

This introductory declaration contains in a nutshell the contradiction to which my further analysis is devoted.

How Sartre interprets his own evolution towards Marxism is of considerable sociological and psychological interest. He was attracted by the force of the Labour Movement; as an intellectual, he was influenced by the rising class whose consciousness is moulded by its own social position. Husserl and Heidegger officiated at the cradle of *L'Etre et le Néant;* but in the *Critique* Sartre had arrived at the conviction that Marxism is the philosophy relevant to our time ("undated"). Anti-Marxism, he states, faces the Hobson's choice of either returning to pre-Marxist ideas or of rediscovering ideas already refuted by Marxism. This is an excellent and terse expression of an important fact many times observed in practice. Various critics have believed themselves to be superseding Marx when in reality they were only harking back to his precursors.

Sartre's ideas on revisionism are of interest. The term is, he says, either a truism or an absurdity. It is a truism when it asserts the evolution of Marxist ideas. That evolution is a necessity even for those who wish to be the most faithful disciples, since Marxism is a living philosophy which changes and grows with the development of society. Revisionism becomes an absurdity when it sets out to make a change in philosophy—which in its opinion finds itself in a state of crisis—by calling in the advise of "experts". If there is a crisis, and if any change is needed, that fact reflects a deeper social crisis, which can only be overcome as a result of social development. A revision made by "experts" is only a mystification. This thought of Sartre goes far beyond the shallow but loud propaganda of the revisionist miracle-makers, and in my opinion deserves a deeper analysis.

So we see that Sartre not only avows Marxist philosophy but attempts to defend it from attack. He ends his introductory study with a far-reaching prognosis of the fusion of Existentialism with Marxism:

> "When Marxist analysis accepts human dimensions (i. e. the Existentialist programme) as the basis of anthropological science, Existentialism loses its reason for existence..."

Is this not too good to be true? Doubts are at once raised by what Sartre says in continuation:

> "...absorbed, mastered and retained by an integrated philosophical movement, it (Existentialism) ceases to be a particular analysis in order to become the basis of every analysis."

Thus Existentialism will "disappear", not in the sense of being overcome by Marxism, which resolves the Existentialist problems in its own way, but by being taken over by Marxism as the basis of every analysis. This is not a case of "disappearance" at all, but of the promotion of Existentialism to the role of serving as the foundation of all Marxist theory. It is a question of "completing" Marxism by Existentialism.

Is such a "completion" possible without giving rise to internal contradictions within the system?

To a certain extent Sartre himself is aware of contradiction. Indeed, in a polemic with Lukacz he once charged the latter with not seeing the contradiction.

"... we were at the same time persuaded that historical materialism provided the only correct interpretation of history and that Existentialism remains the only concrete approach to reality. I do not intend to deny the contradictions inherent in this position. I only say that Lucacz did not suspect them. Further, many intellectuals and many students have lived and still live under the pressure of this post-war exigency. Where does this come from? It results from a circumstance of which Lucacz was well aware but of which he could not say anything at that time: Marxism—which attracts us as the moon does the tides, which has transformed all our ideas and eliminated for us the categories of bourgeois thought—could not satisfy our speculative needs; on the particular ground we occupied it had nothing new to tell us, since it was retarded in its own development."

Sartre is right, of course: there *are* contradictions here. Historical Materialism understands human actions and motives as socially conditioned, whereas Existentialism seeks the true source of social phenomena in the autonomous, free individual. These are two diametrically opposed conceptions which cannot be united. Nor was this accomplished by Sartre, who perhaps managed to insinuate a little Existentialism into Marxism while trying to transform Marxism into a variety of Existentialism. It is not surprising that this new system splits at the seams under pressure of its internal contradictions. In a review of Sartre's book in *Prévues*, under the significant title *Marxism Existentialised*, Aimé Pari rightly remarked that Sartre had sacrificed none of his own doctrines for the sake of the "undated" philosophy, and that his position simply subordinates what he calls Marxism to Existentialism.

The discoveries of Historical Materialism advanced socialism from utopia to science. The discovery of the real mechanism of social development, and in particular of the determining role of the mode of production for the whole of social life, demonstrated the necessity of socialism and identified the social force which could bring it about. The guiding thought of Historical Materialism, and of the whole conception of Scientific Socialism, was historical determinism, which interprets the behaviour of social classes and of human individuals in the light of the discovered laws of social development. Historical Materialism does not deny the role of the individual in history. On the contrary, it strongly emphasises that history is made by people. But it brings out the role of other factors, which determine in the last analysis why people think and act in one way and not in another. Materialism differs from idealism in understanding human thinking not as the primary but as a secondary and derivative factor in making history. True, in taking up this idea so-called sociological science failed to digest it properly. Yet the acceptance of Historical Materialism does involve the recognition of historical determinism and its corollary—the derivative character of the mode of thought in relation to the mode of production. Sartre, however, who declares his avowal of Marxism in the form of Historical Materialism, rejects what is the foundation stone of that materialism, namely, historical determinism with its specific conceptions of the laws of social development, of the derivative character of social consciousness, and of the dialectic inherent in understanding the individual as both the product and at the same time the maker of society.

Is Sartre therefore dishonest in his pro-Marxist declarations? Nothing of the sort. It is simply a matter of contradictions in his views and personal convictions. He gets along with these the easier because he practices philosophy "artistically"—which means with complete carelessness regarding the precise meaning of the words he uses. With deep conviction he declares that vagueness should be the characteristic of every analysis. For the Polish reader, reared in the cult of temperance, clarity and precision of thought—and perhaps for the English reader too—such playing with words is often unbearable.

Here is how Sartre conceives the subject matter of Existentialism:

> "The subject of Existentialism—consequent upon the avoidance of the matter by Marxists—is the individual person in a social environment... the alienated individual transformed into a mere object, mystified, who was created by the division of labour and exploitation, but who struggles against alienation with insufficient means and, in spite of everything, patiently climbs to ever new positions."

It must be acknowledged that this is a proper subject for analysis, and we cannot object if Sartre takes this point of departure for his investigation of dialectical reason, since he clearly stipulates that the individual must be understood socially and as socially conditioned. However, when Sartre proceeds from general declarations to the concrete application of his intentions he arouses serious misgivings. He clearly formulates these methodological intentions in the chapter entitled "Dogmatic and Critical Dialectics".

Here he is concerned with the problem of the freedom of the individual, basic for every variety of Existentialism, which he approaches from the aspect of the relations between the individual and society, the individual and his environment in the broad meaning of the term. There are certain necessities, says Sartre, which the environment imposes on the individual in the form of laws. But the individuals at the same time make history. Such is his dialectic. But inconsistency arises here, since Existentialism desires at all costs to preserve its doctrine of absolute individual freedom—which is at the very heart of Existentialism as a philosophy, and without which it loses its reason for existence. Sartre finds himself entangled in the inconsistencies of an Existentialism which recognises, at least in words, the social conditioning of the individual personality. And he emerges rather too easily from this entanglement. He simply withdraws with his right hand what he grasps with his left. He recognises social conditioning and the necessity flowing from it only in order at once to deny it—"dialectically". This is a poor kind of "dialectic", the defects of which are due, among other things, to the fact that he never even attempts to make precise for himself what he understands by "dialectics" and "contradiction", although he uses these terms incessantly.

> "Man makes history on the basis of the conditions he finds at hand. If that statement is true, it definitively erases determinism and analytical reasoning as a method and rule of human history."

The above-quoted argument of Sartre contains an obvious *non sequitur;* for the statement that people make their own history on the basis of given circumstances does not lead to the erasure of historical determinism but rather to the specific interpretation of the mechanism by which that determinism operates. But Sartre desires at all costs to save the "freedom" of the individual, as understood by Existentialism, the conception of which is required to "complete" Marxism. On this conception of "freedom" rests his understanding of dialectical reasoning, which proceeds beyond what already exists to what does not yet exist but is projected by human activity. Sartre speaks of the dialectic of freedom and necessity, of the dialectic of the external conditioning to which we are subjected, as well as of the dialectic which we ourselves create. It is all terribly hazy and inconsistent. But it does express his intention, as does the following statement:

"...there exists no dialectic that could be imposed on facts, as Kant's categories were imposed on phenomena; dialectical development, if it takes place, is the individual adventure of the particular object."

This is a poetic rather than a philosophical statement. But its intent is clear. Talk as much as you like about "social conditioning", but without the "freedom" of the individual, in the sense of his being free from the action of determinism, Existentialism simply ceases to exist as a philosophical current. This is why determinism must go!

In the name of Existentialism, Sartre demands recognition of the details of historical events, rejecting the idea of laws governing historical development. But without recognising such laws there is no Marxism, no Historical Materialism. Sartre does not particularly care how loose his language is, although the subject requires accuracy of expression. He says further:

"Historical Materialism exists, and the law of that materialism is dialectics. But if, as certain authors maintain, by dialectical materialism if understood some kind of monism which wishes to direct human history from without, then it must be stated that there does not exist, or does not yet exist, any dialectical materialism."

Sartre is, of course, aware that the Existentialist individual with his "freedom" cannot be derived from any Marxist conceptions. Instead, he tries to make the transition from that individual to society, from freedom to necessity, from Existentialism to Marxism, by dragging in the concept of scarcity. He speaks of *rareté*—but the literal translation of the word as "rarity" does not express what he actually has in mind, namely, the lack or inadequacy of means to satisfy human needs. And here there arises a very serious misunderstanding; for Sartre—in all good faith, no doubt—now replaces Marxism with a version of Social Darwinism.

"Certainly," writes Sartre, "however it may be with people and events, they have thus far appeared only within the framework of scarcity, i. e. within the framework of a society still incapable of freeing itself from the domination of its needs, and hence of nature, and which in this connection possesses limited techniques and instruments; a society torn asunder, overwhelmed by its needs and dominated by production, arousing antagonism between the individuals composing it; abstract relations between things, commodities and money, etc., are the premise and condition of direct relations between people; in this manner, implements, the circulation of commodities, etc., determine economic and social development."

Here Sartre tries to make economic scarcity the foundation of the whole mechanism of social development, including the class struggle. Human activity, he says, is carried on within the framework of scarcity of the means of subsistence; hence there is a surplus of population, and people naturally find themselves in antagonistic relations of competition with others for the division of the scarce means of satisfying their needs. The affinity of this with Social Darwinism and Malthusianism is evident—but Sartre mistakes it for Marxism, with which it has nothing whatever in common. The Marxist conception of exploitation and surplus value is based on the fact that the worker produces *more* than the minimum amount required for his own satisfaction according to his historically determined living standards. The social problem in the United States today, for example, where the full employment of existing productive capacity would make possible the immediate transition to the communist principle of distribution according to need, does not consist of any inadequacy in material means; and the class struggle there is certainly not waged within any framework of scarcity. Marxism opposes the ideas of Social Darwinism and Malthusianism, and sees in them merely the apologetics of capitalism which imposes poverty amidst plenty.

The proposed marriage of Marxism and Existentialism cannot, then, be celebrated. Materialism and idealism cannot come together, and no kind of "dialectic" can unite them. Sartre has suffered the fate of many "completers" of Marxism before him, and has entirely failed as a "renewer" of Marxism.

But the fiasco of this marriage does not alter the fact, emphasised earlier, that some of the problems posed by Sartrist Existentialism are important problems. The failure of Sartre's hopeless attempt to reconcile the irreconcilable does not make their discussion any less urgent. Marxism cannot become one with Existentialism, but it can and must defeat it by tackling on its own ground those problems which constitute the vital part of Existentialism.

PART TWO

A PHILOSOPHY OF MAN

5

HUMAN DESTINY AS A SUBJECT
FOR PHILOSOPHY

What is the meaning of life? Is man free to choose
between alternative lines of action? What does it mean
for man to be free to make decisions? Of what consists
an individual's responsibility for his decisions, particularly in situations of conflict? What is one to do in
situations where every decision leads to results considered right from one point of view and wrong from
another? What does the evaluation of our actions depend
on, and how well grounded are such evaluations? How
should we live so that our actions may be evaluated
positively? What is the status of the individual in society
and in the world surrounding him?

Such are a few of the long list of questions which for
some are merely a bunch of pseudo-problems, and for
others constitute not only the heart but the exclusive
concern of philosophy. We need not look far back in
history to find representatives of these two extreme
viewpoints: at the one pole are the Neo-Positivists, at
the other the Existentialists. Here we have a division of
philosophies which enables at least some philosophers to
entertain the conviction, not very flattering to their own
pursuit, that the history of philosophy is a history of
stupidities. Indeed, since philosophers on both sides of
the fence hold this same conviction, it may be suggested
that all of them are right—and in a certain sense this is

true. It would be good if every philosopher would allow himself at least a grain of scepticism about his own position, though this is perhaps to ask too much.

The division among philosophers in relation to the above questions has its historical roots. I have already referred to the historical division between the Ionian and Socratic philosophies. The Ionians initiated the idea that the universal laws governing all the varied phenomena of the world constitute the theme of philosophy. Socrates, as Cicero expressed it, directed philosophy to the hearth, seeing as its theme the quest for proper living. He was not the first to do this, but he upheld this point of view with extreme stubborness and his historical fame justifies naming the whole trend after him. Both these trends have been active throughout the history of philosophy, although they have seldom appeared in a pure form in which one side would completely contradict the other. The case of Neo-Positivism on the one side, and Existentialism on the other, are somewhat exceptional in this respect.

Are the questions I have listed justifiable from the standpoint of philosophy? Is it justifiable to include the destiny of the individual, his behaviour and the evaluation of his behaviour, within the subject matter of philosophy?

The right of philosophy to deal with such questions may be considered from the point of view of their importance to people. Are these merely artificial or contrived questions, arising from speculations detached from living human interests and needs? It is in this sense that we may speak of the speculative or metaphysical character of such questions as how many angels can dance on the point of a needle. But questions about the meaning of life or the freedom of decision are of an entirely different nature to this, although the answers to them often fly off into the clouds of speculation and metaphysics. The questions themselves are indeed most firmly anchored in human practice, and there perhaps exist no questions more real for man than those concerned with proper living. From this point of view, these question are undoubtedly proper questions for philosophy.

On the other hand, we may approach the matter from the angle which mainly interests the opponents of treating the destiny of man as a subject for philosophy. The questions may flow from real human cares and needs, they may be anchored in human practice—but is it possible to answer them scientifically? For a philosophy professing to be scientific, this type of question may be rejected as badly posed and therefore insoluble. Let us look into this more closely.

What makes a philosophy scientific? Two alternative criteria may be suggested. Either the scientific character of the system depends on the truth of its propositions, or it depends on the applicability to them of methods of verification.

If the first alternative is adopted, then the further question arises as to whether the propositions of the system are absolutely or relatively true—"relatively true" meaning partially true in accordance with the historical limitations of human knowledge at a given time.

The pretention to absolute truth is peculiar to metaphysical systems of speculative philosophy, and is so implausible in the light of the development of modern science that no philosophy nowadays would seriously make such a claim. As for relative truth, it becomes difficult to deny the relative truth of particular propositions of different systems, and controversy revolves rather around the question of the adequacy of the world view as a whole. Such a question becomes very hard indeed to decide—for what are the criteria for deciding the degree of truth of a general world view? At any rate, the attempt to justify any proposition of philosophy on grounds of "relative truth" can easily lead to subjectivism and is very dangerous from a scientific point of view.

The second alternative would make a philosophy scientific in so far as actual procedures of scientific investigation are relevant to what it says. Only that philosophy would then be regarded as scientific the propositions of which are constructed as generalisations of the findings of particular branches of science, and which itself investigates the theoretical and methodological foundation of those branches of science. In that case, various different and rival philosophies could all retain a scientific character. The field of discussion and conflict in philosophy becomes tremendously wide and, taking the development of science itself into account, uniformity is hardly to be expected. This approach does open up some perspective for the solution of the problems we are discussing here.

Obviously, to ask questions about, say, determinism in the processes of the material world, and about "the meaning of life", means inquiring into matters which are not only different but most be differently treated.

In the first case, the scientific character of given philosophical propositions depends on their relation to the contemporary findings of the various branches of science—physics, biology, and so on. Certain German philosophers once declared that if reality did not accord with their philosophical systems, so much the worse for reality. They would hardly find supporters now. Philosophy has to be in agreement with the sciences. Of course, philosophical interpretations may differ, especially in relation to scientific findings which are not yet uniformly agreed, or where there is a lack of intermediary links for proceeding from established facts to philosophical generalisations. The lack of such links is, indeed, rather characteristic here; and Russell is correct in his assertion that philosophy ends where complete precision and confirmation begins.

Is the situation similar with questions about the meaning of life, freedom of choice, the relation of the individual to society, and so on?

Yes and no. Yes, when there exist the scientifically established data of some specific science. No, because the questions themselves are hazy and ambiguous, and it not clear to which particular branch of science to turn in trying to answer them.

But that does not make the questions pseudo-questions. As long as people die, suffer, lose their dear ones, so long will questions arise about the meaning of life—which must be understood, in this case as about the values of life and why one should not be allowed to put an end to suffering at will. As long as people continue to confront life situations which contain conflicts and in which they must take decisions and act, often inflicting harm on some people by doing good to others, so long will there be questions as to how to live properly and how to make decisions in such situations. So long as people desiring to attain their ends encounter in society the contrary desires of other people, so long will there be questions about the limits to one's freedom of choice and the relation of the individual to society. These are question of a different type to, say, the question of determinism, and must be differently approached. But they are not pseudo-questions.

The fact is that philosophy may entertain a variety of questions, which have to be answered in different ways, and the answers will have varying degrees of scientific warranty depending upon the extent of the scientific exploration of a given field. When the accumulation of scientific knowledge treaches a cerain point, when a proposition is verified by means of the methods of a definite branch of science, then the problem passes out of the competence of philosophy and becomes the subject of a definite branch of science. It is in this way that individual problems and entire complexes of problems have dropped off, and continue to drop off, the common trunk of philosophy. If any philosopher then continues to attack such problems with the aid of the philosophical imagination he simply encroaches into the field of a given branch of science, and his efforts are worse than useless. Thus, for example, the whole traditional *Naturphilosophie*, the domain of a-priori reasoning, has perished—although philosophers continue today to deal with the themes of the natural sciences, particularly in their methodological aspects.

Subject to the above reservation, every theme of a sufficient level of generalisation may legitimately be the subject of one or another branch of philosophy. The Neo-Positivist proposal to remove from the domain of philosophy the whole subject of traditional ethics with its collateral problems of the individual and his destiny, is just as absurd as the efforts of certain Existentialists to forbid philosophy from interesting itself in questions arising from the natural sciences—which would rule out problems of ontology and the theory of knowledge. It is characteristic, by the way, that in their crusades against "metaphysics" both sides become swamped by their own metaphysics. In both cases the crusade is doomed to failure from the start, since real problems cannot be exorcised even by the most potent incantations.

6

THE MEANING OF LIFE

Faced with such a hazy question as "What is the meaning of life?" it is necessary first of all to try to make the question more precise. There are perhaps two main interpretations of this question. He who asks about the meaning of life questions first of all the value of life: is life worth living? And secondly, he questions the aim of life.

"Is life worth living?" is a common question, whether the questioner seriously proposes to draw practical conclusions from a negative answer, or whether he asks in the hope of cheering himself up. The Stoics maintained that it is not necessary to console people over the inevitability of death; on the contrary, they must be persuaded that it worth while to go on living.

However that may be, death—the threat of one's own death and the death of near ones—is often the chief incentive for reflections on the meaning of life. For besides peoples' dread of dying, they experience the tragedy of separation in the actual deaths of those close to them. People fear dying as a possibility, and experience the death of someone near to them as an actuality. We are only sometimes reminded of the inevitable approach of our own death; if it were otherwise, if people lived with the continual consciousness of death inevitably approaching, they would surely go mad. We feel the passage of time, like the flow of blood in the veins, only occasionally. Nikolaj Kuzmicz, in Rilke's *Laurid Brigge's*

Malta Notebook, could live no longer once he became conscious of the passage of time.

But the question "Is life worth living?" is suggested not only by death. Physical as well as moral suffering— particularly when it seems undeserved—prompts the same question. How can such a question be answered? And how can we explain our answer to others?

We would like to answer: although death is inevitable, although suffering is unavoidable, life is still worth while, life has a meaning. But why? We are obliged to say why, if we are to convince anyone and if our answer is to express anything more than an individual opinion.

The ground we are moving on now becomes excessively slippery, and a different mode of approach is needed from that adopted towards problems in the exact or empirical sciences, or towards epistemological and ontological problems arising from the sciences. We can speak of certainties in deductive sciences and probabilities in empirical sciences which differ in degree but are always based on hard data. This also applies, though in a different way, to propositions of the philosophy of science. But with the questions we are now discussing it is not a matter of ascertaining the truth or falsity of propositions, but of assessing, evaluating. It is doubtful whether there can ever be a valid transition from description to evaluation. It is doubtful whether a description of life, however true and well founded, would automatically justify any evaluation of life.

At this point a Neo-Positivist may interject that evaluations cannot express facts and cannot be verified, so that all evaluation is subjective. He would undoubtedly be right. But he would at the same time be wrong if he concluded that questions of evaluation were pseudo-questions and so refused to deal with them. In that case he would simply be assuming what has to be proved; he would be assuming a criterion of meaningfulness and scientific character which would prejudge the problem from the start.

Actually, in examining questions such as the meaning of life, the philosopher must proceed quite differently from any procedure of the natural sciences. He must proceed differently because the subject that interests him demands a different procedure. But it does not follow that his method is impermissible, or necessarily unscientific. He, too, generalises from the facts of experience; he too bases himself on the findings of specific sciences, such as sociology or psychology. But he proceeds differently, because he does not simply describe but assesses, evaluates. And where an assessment or evaluation is being made, some scale of assessment, some chosen system of values, enters into his calculations. Of course, the selection of this scale or system is not made arbitrarily: it is socially conditioned. But social conditioning is not the only factor. Other factors come into play as well, both psychological and physiological, which belong to the individual's own personality. In one way or another such factors will always make themselves felt whenever there is a question of choice, including choice of a world view. And not only intellectual factors are involved here, but emotional factors. Hence subjectivity does play its part.

Consequently, the process of generalisation is also different. The gap between established empirical facts and their philosophical generalisation is greater; and therefore the possibility of varied interpretation is also greater. In this field the philosopher resembles the ancient sage musing over human life, rather than the experimental natural scientist. This is so, simply because the procedures of the natural scientist are useless here. The philosopher who devotes himself to questioning the meaning of life is not proceeding scientifically—but that does not imply that he is unscientific. The alternative "scientific-unscientific" does not apply here, and to call the philosopher "unscientific" would, logically, be like concluding that love is not rectangular from a negative answer to the question whether love is rectangular.

A wise man is not the same as a scholar, though scholarship and wisdom may often go together. A scholar is one who possesses a fund of knowledge in some field; he is erudite in that field. But one is wise to the extent that he is intelligent and experienced, particularly in his dealings with others. Some people are scholars in some special field but are not wise, either in the sense of general intelligence or of experience of life and knowledge of how to get on with other people. And vice versa, some people are wise without possessing erudition. The philosophy of one who engages in the problems we are concerned with should be classed as "wise" or "unwise", as suitable or unsuitable, but not as "scientific" or "unscientific". In certain situations it is a person wise in the ways of life who is most needed. So a philosopher should be not only a scholar but a wise man too. This does not contradict the requirement that he should be scientific. Scientific knowledge, the scientific approach, helps with reflections on human life and with defining an attitude towards life. The answer proposed to problems such as "What is the meaning of life?" depends, as we have seen, on various factors, but primarily on the world view of the person reflecting on the question; and such a world view may be scientific or unscientific.

For the religious believer, the question whether life has a meaning and is worth living is answered very simply, because even suffering, pain and death are in accord with the will of a higher being, who has prepared rewards in the hereafter for the faithful and punishment for transgressors. For the believer, the most difficult problems appear very simple. But a high price has to be paid for this convenience; it is bought only at the cost of a scientific attitude.

It is not possible from a lay standpoint to provide any kind of categorical and universal answer to the question whether life is worth while. Whether it is worth while or not for a given individual depends upon his actual conditions and perspectives of life—and the individual concerned has the last word here. He can draw up a kind of balance sheet, recalling everything in his life which he evaluates positively, and reminding himself of what he may easily forget under emotional strain—that he lives only once, that time alleviates suffering, that he has responsibilities to those close to him and to society, and so on. But only he can sum up the balance. For if one does not accept absolute standards, which are in essence religious, one cannot prejudge the answers for each individual. That would mean making a choice for him, which only he can make.

But he who asks whether life is worth while asks at the same time about the aim of life. What do we live for? This question is put by everyone harassed by the problem of how he should live. For our behaviour, especially in situations of conflict, depends on what we consider to be the aim of life. This remains true whether we have consciously formulated for ourselves an aim of life or not; for an idea of the aim of life, induced by education in the broadest sense of the word, is implicit in human behaviour. This applies alike to the hero who dedicates his life to the defense of some ideal, the traitor who collaborates with the enemy for money, the conscientious man who sacrifices his own interests to what he considers to be right, or the opportunist who accommodates himself to his superiors despite his own convictions.

From a religious standpoint the question of the aim of life is answered very simply. Man is subject to an external purpose, that of God, which he should obey. The only problem is to find out what this purpose is—

which is done by study of the scriptures or other records of revelation. The argument against this standpoint must seek to demonstrate scientifically the human origin of these revelations, to show that God does not create man but man creates God in his own image. But of course, there can be no argument against a believer who will not accept the canons of scientific demonstration.

Lay answers to the question of the aim of life are various, and have long since been classified within the history of philosophy. So far as general approach is concerned, it is now difficult to think of anything new, except for new names. It is an "eternal question", concerning the answers to which we may feel inclined to agree that "there is nothing new under the sun". Yet the moment we stop limiting ourselves to merely abstract and general characterisation of views, and begin to penetrate deeply into the social conditions required for realising one or another aim of our activity, the situation changes. Marxist theory, like several very different ontological and epistemological theories, leads to the general position that may be called "social hedonism"—the view that the aim of human life is to secure the maximum happiness for the broadest masses of the people, and that only within the compass of this aim can personal happiness be realised. But taking into account the social conditions required to realise this aim, the Marxist avows socialist humanism as his supreme principle. Socialist humanism is indeed a variety of "social hedonism". But it is a concretised conception so closely connected with all the other tenets of Marxism that its admission implies the acknowledgement of the whole system.

The propositions of socialist humanism and its precepts for behaviour flow from the theory of Historical Materialism, and in particular: (1) the specific understanding of the individual as a social product—as a product of "the totality of social relations", of which we shall say more later; (2) the specific understanding of the relation of the individual to society on the basis of the historical materialist conception of social development; (3) the recognition that ideals can be realised only under given social conditions, without which recognition they degenerate into utopias. All this leads, not to abstract ideals, but to scientifically based concepts from which flow definite and practical conclusions in the from of precepts for behaviour.

The socialist humanist is persuaded that he can find personal happiness only through the happiness of society. For only broader horizons for personal development and enlarged possibilities for the satisfaction of human desires on a social scale create the necessary foundations for realising personal aspirations. He does not limit himself to seeking relations of friendship or love with those near him—although that is closest to his heart. He understands that the realisation of his aspirations demands struggle, that the cause he serves is socially conditioned and requires definite changes in social relations. In a society based on social antagonism he understands that the realisation of his aspirations demands changes in property relations and in the class relations based on them. He advocates the class struggle in the name of the love of near ones and of universal friendship, and he proclaims his hatred of the exploitation of man by man in the name of love of man.

The socialist humanist knows that man is the product of social conditions, but he also knows that these conditions were created by man. He is a dialectician, and, precisely because of that, fights while proclaiming peace. His ideal of socialism is at one with his humanism. As an ideal, socialism is the consistent expression of humanism; at the same time, socialism is the material realisation of the ideal of humanism. For this cause, the socialist humanist is ready to make the greatest sacrifices, and to appeal to others to do the same. He accepts the precept of "love thy neighbour", and has only contempt for those who proclaim this beautiful precept in words and betray it in deeds. For socialist humanism not only proclaims certain ideals but calls for struggle to implement them in life, and to convince other people of the necessity of joining this struggle.

7

FREEDOM AND HISTORICAL NECESSITY

We have defined socialist humanism as a fighting humanism. It advocates struggle to realise an aim in life, to transform social relations as a condition for realising that aim, to win people for that aim and so change their former attitudes. But can all that be done? Can man, as a product of society, be himself the creator of social life? Does not historical necessity, as recognised by Marxism, contradict the individual's freedom and nullify his will to struggle?

In my opinion, two main questions are involved here. The first concerns the status of the individual—the central question in the argument with Existentialism. The second concerns the extent to which the individual determines his own destiny.

Discussion in this field has traditionally had a scholastic character, and it has, moreover, been full of semantic confusions—meaningless or ambiguous posing of questions, and the use of vague, ambiguous words.

On the one hand, so-called determinists have often limited themselves to pointing out that human actions, like everything else in the world, have causes, are causally determined. This reduces the question of the freedom of the individual to the question of whether any human activity is purely spontaneous or uncaused. Answering that nothing happens without a cause, these determinists find themselves denying human freedom and involved in a fatalistic view of human affairs.

On the other hand, opponents of determinism have often confined themselves to stating obvious facts, such as—handed a glass of water, one may drink it or not, as one chooses; arriving at a cross roads, one may turn right or left as one chooses; and so on.

On such a level, discussion about determinism and freedom is cheap and easy. But deeper questions are involved than appear from such merely verbal exchanges. First of all, the question of the freedom of the individual is discussed as though the concept of the individual were itself clear, whereas it is in fact surrounded with controversy.

The main source of conflict between Marxism and Sartrist Existentialism lies in the conception of the individual. For Sartre, at any rate for the Sartre of *L'Etre et le Néant*, the individual is an autonomous being absolutely free to dispose of his own destiny, and therefore lonely and condemned to freedom. Consequently he lives in continual inner torment. This conception seems very odd to anyone acquainted with the most elementary facts of sociology or psychology. True, in *Critique de la Raison Dialectique* Sartre begins to accept some of the findings of sociology—but that emphasises the fact that his standpoint is riddled with contradictions.

To open the debate, I would like to replace the Existentialist thesis about the individual's "isolation" with the completely contrary proposition that the individual is from birth to death connected most closely with other people—that he is a deeply social being, socially conditioned in every aspect of his existence, even in his most intimate experiences. In the light of contemporary knowledge, this proposition is in a certain sense trivial, and I present it as such. But in this very triviality lies the sharpest criticism of its adversaries. Of course, people are often lonely—without quotation marks; but that fact gives no support to the philosophical notion of man's absolute "loneliness". Actually, the important problem is not that of refuting this philosophical notion, but is that of limiting and overcoming the apparent fettering of the individual by society.

It is easy to demonstrate the determining influence of society on man's psychology, on his views, and consequently on his values and his manner of arriving at decisions and choosing what to do. But the essence of the question lies much deeper. It is that of discovering the implications of the fact that man is always and everywhere the product of society and, in a certain sense, the reflection of social relations. This is what the young Marx had in mind when he wrote in the *Theses on Feuerbach*: "The human essence is no abstraction inherent in each single individual. In its reality it is the ensemble of the social relations."

Already in the seventeenth century John Locke struck a blow against "the abstract human essence". Man, he declared, is not born with innate ideas, with innate moral sentiments, attitudes and habits. These are formed in man under the influence of social upbringing.

First of all comes the influence of language, the first social acquirement imprinted upon the child's mind, in the vocabulary and syntax of which are embedded society's accumulated knowledge of the world, bequeathed to each of its members by education. The system of language shapes the system of thought, the way in which people understand the world through the classification of the phenomona of the world. And through the intermediary of language man's whole mentality and attitude takes shape. Man cannot jump out of his social framework. Even as a pioneer, a rebel and destroyer of the existing order, he is entangled in given social relations, which he himself created.—Evidently, then, Jehovah was right to have prohibited anyone born in slavery from entering the Promised Land, which was to be a land of freedom.

Language, beliefs, knowledge, customs, moral sentiments, tastes, political convictions, personal traits—all issue from given social relations, for all are concerned with definite forms of co-operation amongst human beings. From his birth, a man finds himself within a given social system, and he cannot choose which system to be born into. He lives in and by means of a social environment which moulds him and makes him what he is. Precisely this is the meaning of Marx's statement that the human essence—that is, what all men have in common and which distinguishes man from the rest of the animal world—is the ensemble of social relations.

The individual is socially conditioned, a product of the ensemble of social relations—such is the conclusion. And this implies that the individual is not the starting point but rather the final end for our inquiry. However, the dialectics of his situation comes into play here. The individual is at the same time a product and a producer; he is at once the end result and the starting point. The whole difficulty of comprehending the role and problems of the individual arises from this dialectic. But once this dialectic is grasped, there falls to the ground the subjectivist idea of Existentialism—that the individual, as the maker of society and history, is an absolute starting point for any inquiry, requiring no sort of investigation or clarification. Like Descartes' *cogito*[1], how supposedly simple is the Existentialists' *homo agens*! There is no need for any further analysis of the foundations on which is erected their whole construction, with its categories of freedom, condemnation to choose, loneliness, fear, and so on! But unfortunately the construction has no foundation, not because *homo agens* does not exist, but because his existence is different from what they claim. He does not exist as an isolated individual autonomous in his choices

---

[1] The French philosopher René Descartes put forward the proposition *cogito ergo sum*, "I think therefore I am", as the absolute certainty from which everything else had to be deduced.

and decisions which depend on his own "free will" alone. He does not exist as a Leibnizian monad, "without any windows"[2], who can receive no advice or help from anywhere. On the contrary, man as an individual is never alone, since even his loneliest thoughts are socially formed and conditioned. His decisions and choices are always socially conditioned, and so he is never "free" in the Existentialist sense of this term.

Da liegt der Hund begraben! That's where the trouble lies. The whole Existentialist idea of freedom, the whole anti-determinist furore, all the pretentions of Sartre and his friends to agree with Marxism about objective laws governing social development because these laws result from the sum of accidental individual actions—all arise from the Existentialist idea of the "free" individual. This idea is quite arbitrary. It owes nothing to any scientific investigation of man or society, contradicts the findings of every investigation, and has simply been dug up out of the philosophical old curiosity shop. For it is true that the fundamental idea of this super-stylish and ultra-modern philosophy is inexorably dated and smells of mothballs. It needed the extreme philosophical ignorance and complete political chaos which reigned at one time amongst some of the intellectuals in our country for them to become enraptured by the "originality" of ideas which were faithfully copied from the Existentialist model. Perhaps the only basis for this phenomenon was that anyone who spoke up against Marxism then passed for an original thinker.

I will not consider here the question of the objective character of the laws governing human history. True, it is related to the questions under discussion but it

---

[2] G. W. Leibniz, codiscoverer with Newton of the differential calculus, thought that the world consisted of "simple spiritual substances" or "monads", each a completely independent being and none of which could act on any other. He expressed this by saying that "the monad has no windows".

presents a separate problem in the field of the theory and methology of modern science which calls for a different kind of analysis. In the present context, we are interested in something else — whether within the operation of objective laws governing the development of society there remains any place where man is free to shape his own social life. This brings me to the second problem which was proposed for discussion. And in order to deal with it, it becomes necessary to begin by clearing away some misunderstandings arising from using the word "freedom" in various different senses.

When we speak of "freedom" what we usually mean is the opposite of constraint. In this sense, a man is free when not constrained by physical or other external forces. A man is not free when some external constraint denies him the possibility of choice—even though this constraint may be for his own good. No-one likes to be constrained, and so everyone is in favour of being free, in the sense of not being constrained.

But when we speak of "free will" as incompatible with "determinism", we must evidently be referring to something else than merely freedom from constraint. For the fact that you are not constrained by external forces does not imply that there is no cause determining what you do. Not everyone, however, understands this; and even when it is understood there remains a purely emotional revulsion against any suggestion that the will is "determined". So people still think that "determinism" denies "freedom". This comes from a simple logical fallacy—the mixing up of different senses of the same word.

We should in fact distinguish three meanings of the word "freedom":

1) A man is free when his will to act is not determined by anyone or anything.

2) A man is free when his activity is not subordinated to any objective necessities of social life or historical development.
3) A man is free when he is able to choose one of several alternative courses of action.

Those who discuss "freedom" usually concentrate on the first and second meanings. But in my opinion the real problem is connected with the third meaning.

The tendency to contrast individual freedom with determinism is fully understandable in those who adopt an Existentialist conception of the individual. They wish to assert "absolute" freedom, in the sense of indeterminism, absence of any determining causes, in the sphere of operation of the human will. This kind of indeterminism is, indeed, a major ingredient in the subjectivist conception of the individual. But the mixing up of freedom with indeterminism is a hoary fallacy, which cannot withstand a breath of criticism. The identification of freedom with the action of a will which is absolutely undetermined assumes that there are events which have no causes. For this identification implies that voluntary actions are such uncaused events. But such an assumption can be made only by a mystic for whom plain evidence has no value. There is no evidence for uncaused voluntary action; on the contrary, every study of human activity shows that there are causes for what people do.

There is a more modest and sober variety of indeterminism, however, associated with our second sense of the word "freedom". This view maintains that the freely-acting individual is not subordinated to any objective necessities of social life or historical development. And although it rests on a misunderstanding, this version of indeterminism does pose an important problem, namely: how far is the individual the independent creator of social life and so of his own destiny? And this is a problem which cannot be lightly dismissed.

Are there objective laws of social development and necessities of social life associated with them? As I have already indicated, I do not propose to discuss this question, but to take its answer for granted. Suffice it to say that no serious social scientist today can deny the operation of objective laws of social development, particularly in the economic sphere—and for any who did deny it, all empirical investigation in sociology would be like the labour of Sisyphus. What is more, the role of the economic basis in social development has today become so widely accepted by social and historical science that many appear to have forgotten that the discovery was originally due to Marx. This is certainly a splendid success for the scientific theory of Marxism, in the light of which sneering references to Marxism have a somewhat hollow sound.

Assuming, then, that there are objective laws of social development, does this imply that we cease to be free individuals, because our activity is subordinated to objective social necessities? As usual, it all depends on what we mean by "freedom".

Let us begin with freedom of choice. No-one, not even the most zealous partisans of the objective character of the laws of history, would maintain that these laws determine the decisions and actions of each individual, although they may influence them. No-one would wish to assert that every decision or choice of every individual is determined by objective laws of social development. In general, the laws of social development apply to the results of historical processes, and not to the freedom of action of the individual. People can perform many actions, including actions in opposition to objective tendencies of social development. Those who complain that their freedom is limited or even nullified by the operation of some objective law of history are not therefore really complaining because they are rendered unfree in their actions, but because they cannot obtain by their actions any and every result that they would like. No objective necessity prevents a man from placing whatever bets he likes on horses—but it does prevent him from winning every time.

The standpoint we are discussing amounts, then, to saying that a man is free only when nothing prevents him from being able to get whatever he wants. But this is a crazy conception of freedom.

Our next question is as follows: Is historical necessity an external necessity in relation to the activities of individuals? Is it something imposed from outside upon human activity? To suppose that it is, is a mystical conception which has nothing in common with the views of those who assert the objective character of the laws of social development. Those who make this supposition conduct controversy in a morass of misunderstanding.

Marxist determinism understands historical necessity, not as a force acting on society from outside, independent of society, but as operating precisely through human actions. Men make their own history; but the historical circumstances in which they act and the necessities arising from these circumstances influence their decisions and actions. This involves nothing apart from people, nothing independent of what they do. Nor is there anything mystical about the way the laws of history work out. Changes in the mode of production, for example, simply give rise to certain necessities—and corresponding desires and actions follow in their wake. It is clear that those whose interests suffer from the trend of historical development will tend to fight against it, in their views as in their deeds. But since people's individual attitudes are influenced not only by material interests, the actual social process becomes very complicated. Thus not all those who have a material interest in a given trend of development will support it, and not all those who have not will oppose it. There are socialists and revolutionaries amongst the bourgeosie, and reactionaries and counter-revolutionaries amongst the proletariat. In short, the naive idea of the pre-determination of individual attitudes by class origin has nothing in common with Marxist determinism, with a scientific conception of the operation of objective laws of social development. Yet some incentives are so powerful that ever increasing numbers of people respond to them. What we call necessity is nothing else than the sum of a tremendous number of individual events. In given circumstances, a certain type of attitude and action is bound in time to become predominant amongst a given class of people.

Nothing happens without people. Everything is brought about by people. This implies no violation of people's freedom of action. The best proof that individuals do make their own choices and follow their own bent in relation to social events, independent of historical necessity and in spite of it, is the fact that within every class are to be found revolutionaries, counter-revolutionaries and those who are simply neutral in relation to social conflicts.

The existence of objective laws governing historical development, and of necessity in social processes, neither eliminates men's creative activity nor erases their freedom. These laws only determine the social foundation on which people engage in activity and give expression to their freedom. Certainly, men's activities are limited by social factors. Freedom does not mean the possibility of shaping social processes in whatever way one likes. In this sense, there is no "absolute" freedom, and the conception of it is a mere speculative fantasy. If those who indulge in this fantasy are disillusioned by real life, they have only themselves to blame. Dietzgen once said that believers in "absolute knowledge" had a place only amongst the angels. The same applies to believers in "absolute freedom", who, under the slogan of "all or nothing", scorn the only kind of freedom which is possible for mankind. For the rest of us, the most complete possible kind of freedom is sufficient.

There still remains the third meaning of the word "freedom". If freedom is asserted in this sense, then neither determinism in general nor the operation of objective laws of social development is rejected. Freedom is simply understood as the possibility of choice between different actions in the same situation. This is an extremely modest demand, compared with the fantastic aspirations we have been discussing. For this reason, it accords with the ordinary everyday meaning of the word—freedom from constraint.

When speaking of freedom one ordinarily thinks neither of determinism nor of the operation of objective laws of history, but of situations like the following:

Two camps in society are engaged in conflict, and I am considering which side to be on—for the revolution, or with its opponents. I can decide one way or the other, and I am therefore free. As a free agent, I choose one of the sides, weighing all the pros and cons as they affect me personally and also from a general national and human point of view. Of course, various factors must finally determine my decision, otherwise I could never reach any decision at all. And certainly, the actual operation of objective laws of social development is relevant to my decision—for I try to figure out what the probable results of the conflict and of various actions relating to it will be, and if social events were governed by no laws then it would be impossible to make any predictions of probable events on which to base a decision. But none of this limits my freedom. On the contrary, I can decide only because there *are* factors which determine my decision, only because there *are* objective laws which regulate events in such a way that I can make some estimate as to how they are moving and what the consequences of different actions will be.

It follows that I am free whenever I am able to choose what to do, and when my choice depends on me. In making my choice I act as an individual—but as a real, live individual, a member of society socially conditioned by "the ensemble of social relations", and not as some Existentialist abstraction. I am therefore free on the basis of determinism, within the framework of determinism.

It follows, moreover, that I am free even in situations where I am denied freedom. Of course, this sounds paradoxical only because of different senses in which the word "freedom" is used. But the fact is real and significant. I may be in chains and under the threat of death, but I can still choose—to live as a traitor, or to die honourably. I am still free.

We see, then, that this seemingly narrow and modest conception of freedom is in essence far broader and more significant than its pretentious competitors. Despite fine words, the fantasy of "absolute freedom" leads to nothing but disappointment and resignation, if not despair. It is very evident that in practice such "freedom" has no meaning at all.

To give up fantasies about freedom does not lead to giving up freedom but, on the contrary, to a real understanding of it which can become a mobilising force in the struggle for an ideal. For besides the possibility of choosing not to be imposed upon by others, there is the possibility of choosing not to be imposed upon by oneself—by one's own cowardice, opportunism or self-seeking. No-one can take such freedom away from me, unless I forfeit it myself. The possibility is always there, so that in all eventualities this internal freedom remains. This is something one must learn for oneself, and also teach to others by personal example. This conception of freedom confounds and confutes all the philosophers of despair, all the claptrap about man being "lonely", "condemned to making a choice", and "living in fear". For all its modesty, ours is a strong and far-reaching conception, an affirmation of confidence in man's power and in his social essence.

8

MORAL RESPONSIBILITY AND POLITICS

The problem of individual responsibility at once arises from that of individual freedom. And we may distinguish various kinds of responsibility on the basis of their relation to different kinds of action or of failure to act.

Anyone who agrees to do something and does it badly is, by accepted standards, responsible for the harm done. This is the legal type of responsibility, whether the actual case is formally covered by a law or not. Thus a builder is responsible if the house falls down because it was badly built, a doctor guilty of neglect is responsible for the death of his patient, a railway signalman is responsible if his oversight causes an accident, and so on, and so on.

We often speak, however, of a moral responsibility dissociated from any kind of legal obligation. For example, someone in a state of despair implores you to comfort him, but you do nothing about it. Here a moral responsibility has been shirked, and if the person commits suicide you have a moral responsibility for allowing it to happen.

Many such types of moral responsibility are pretty straightforward and present no special problem. What I shall be concerned with here is moral responsibility in the special kind of situation which created such a ferment amongst us in Poland in 1955—57. This is a problem which came to philosophy straight from life, from political practice—the problem of moral responsibility for political actions in situations of conflict. Here is no simple problem, but a problem of how to behave when there is a conflict between the discipline of an organisation and one's conviction that a given action would be wrong. This is an immense question, which requires frank treatment and calling things by their right names.

I shall define a morally conflicting situation as one where an action which aims at results considered good by an accepted system of values would nevertheless lead to consequences which are bad by the same system. In that case, a person is subject to moral incentives which bid him to act in opposite ways. That is how a moral conflict is created.

To bring to light situations of moral conflict is to strike a blow at general moralising. For this type of moralising is bankrupt in face of morally conflicting situations. The panacea of moral precepts is powerless before the objective barrier to their application. For where the moralist considers his job is done, by citing the commandments and prohibitions, the problem actually begins. It often happens that the fulfillment of a commandment is synonymous with its violation. The problem here is not one of knowing the commandments and prohibitions, but of choosing how to apply them when every choice is a bad one. In that case, it is necessary to choose "the lesser evil". But how is one to decide what is the lesser evil? On the basis of what standards? The religious as the lay moralist is silent on this problem. Both say, for example, "thou shalt not kill". But what am I to do if by refraining from killing a traitor when I have the chance, I send to their deaths my comrades in the underground struggle? It is easy to preach absolute standards, but difficult to resolve real life situations. A morality is worth little which is calculated only to tell thieves that they do wrong, but is inapplicable to the affairs of honest people who desire guidance as to how to live well when situations compel them against their will to do evil.

This, by the way, is why the holy zeal of some of our Polish "ideologists" led them astray recently, and made them miss the essential problem. If one can only repeat that morality takes precedence over politics, one confesses only one's poverty—it does not help in political practice. The problem begins when we desire to determine which *is* the moral way in politics.

Let us then discuss the concrete problem already mentioned—the problem of moral responsibility when the discipline of my party obliges me to act in a way which I believe or even am convinced is wrong.

The discipline of a revolutionary party is no formal question. The obligation to observe it follows from my adherence to the aims of the party, which I voluntarily joined because I was convinced that the party's programme was right. Party discipline is a condition for the success of the party's struggle; without it, the organisation falls apart and becomes ineffective. To accept party discipline is therefore my self-assumed obligation, which I accepted by my own choice when I joined the party. So it is a serious matter for me to think of violating discipline, of refusing to carry out a party decision or, worse, doing something to frustrate it. What are my real reasons for it? Do not my scruples, which are not shared by many party members whom I know to be honest, flow from subjective weaknesses, from lack of experience or resolution? Should I not therefore carry out decisions regardless, cherishing the unity of the party above everything else, despite my misgivings and vacillations?

On the other hand I am consumed with fear that an action which I myself must perform, or at least approve, is wrong precisely from the point of view of the political purpose which is dear to me and for the sake of which I joined the party. I think to myself: this action will militate against the aims of the party, undermine its support, deplete its ranks. And I think this as a member of the party, from the standpoint of its interests. I feel morally responsible for the final outcome.

What to do? If I put discipline first, then I am making my primary moral responsibility that of upholding the unity and discipline of the party at the given time, thereby renouncing my responsibility for the final outcome. If I act in the contrary way, then I am attaching a much greater value to my own consistent attitude in relation to the concrete question than, perhaps, to the aim itself, including its moral side. The conflict here is objective, the choice difficult.

Of course, the stand taken by our "moralisers" had nothing to do with all of the above. Those who simply proclaimed "morality has precedence over politics" did not recognise the moral conflict here, because they maintained that politics is devoid of morality and that there is no moral problem connected with party discipline. Only outsiders could think in such a way, only people who did not regard the party and its discipline as their own. Perhaps this was only a temporary attitude, the result of a political shock. All the same, such was actually their attitude.

In order to make a choice in such situations one ordinarily guides himself by drawing up a balance of gains and losses. But a general table of moral weights and measures is of no avail here, first because situations differ and each has its own concrete character, second because the concrete character of the situation depends partly on how the given person feels about it. It is therefore impossible to express oneself in categorical and absolute terms on such matters.

As in all cases involving individual choice, the final decision can only be made by the individual concerned. No-one can do it for him. But the individual can be helped to choose by pro and con arguments, and advising him how oneself would act in the same situation. Such advice does not release the person himself from the need to make his own choice and from his personal responsibility for it. Still, it can help.

In one sense, the individual is undoubtedly "lonely" here, as the Existentialists have said. He must make the choice himself, and no-one can do it for him. This may even lead to breakdown and catastrophe, when the individual cannot cope with his own inner conflicts. Yet "loneliness" and "being condemned to choose", as understood by the Existentialists, have nothing in common with what happens in reality. For the individual remains conditioned by systems of values and personal patterns which are social in nature, and his reasoning too is socially conditioned when he settles accounts with his conscience in making his choice. In this sense, the individual is never isolated, he is not left to himself and lonely.

To return to our theme of how a decision is to be made, it must be said at once that there is no simple recipe. For those who are sincere and not just formal members of the party we can only say that it depends on taking into account the role of unity and discipline in relation to the realisation of party aims. This approach is based on the assumption—itself of a moral character— that the interests of party unity prevail in the event of a personal doubt, and that personal misgivings must be repressed for the sake of the general cause. But that is only an assumption, not the final solution of every problem. The solution is in each case a matter of the given individual, and can be found only by himself. If one arrives at the subjective certainty that an action is so wrong and harmful as to injure the aims of the party, then moral responsibility demands dissociation from a party decision in the concrete case and action in accordance with one's own conviction. In this case, the individual really is "condemned to make a choice", and our recent experiences show that neither public opinion in general nor opinion within the party can absolve him of responsibility. I could illustrate this with very eloquent examples.

The conflict which appears here is at bottom one between collective discipline and the search for truth. This conflict is very often ignored by us as something to be ashamed of. But that is wrong. It is a human problem, and Marxist theory itself would demonstrate best that human beings, collectively and individually, are bound to be fallible. The cult of infallibility has nothing in in common with Marxism, the founder of which proclaimed methodological scepticism as his basic principle — *de omnibus dubitandum est*, "everything is to be doubted".

Yet there cannot be any conflict between politics and the search for truth, if the politics are truly inspired by Marxism. Of course, there is conflict sometimes between bad, mistaken policies and the organisational discipline involved in their execution, on the one hand, and truth on the other. But the correct politics of the struggle for social progress are based on truth, on the desire and search for truth. It is this consideration which must finally determine the attitude of a creative worker when faced with a conflict between politics and a truth of which his work leaves him in no doubt. This determines his moral and social responsibility, even if that truth is not generally recognised. For what would happen in science and art, and in politics too, if we were permitted to recognise truth only on condition that it was already universally accepted? History affirms that we should then be overwhelmed by intellectual stagnation and dogmatism.

Brecht's philosophical drama, *Galileo*, ends with a shocking monologue, the hero's self-accusation. Old, morally decayed by the consciousness of his cowardice, Galileo refuses the comfort offered by his pupils who are ready to change their opinion about him when they learn that, despite all persecution and dangers, he has completed his scientifically revolutionary *Discorsi* and concealed it from the Inquisition. Galileo is harsher in his judgment on himself than the spectator is inclined to be, and his final words touch the quintessence of what we have here been discussing.

"Even a wool merchant, apart from buying cheaply and selling dear, must also be concerned that trade in wool can be carried on unhindered. In this respect the pursuit of science seems to me to require particular courage. It is concerned with knowledge, achieved through doubt. Making knowledge about everything available for everybody, science strives to make sceptics of them all... I, as a scientist, had a unique opportunity. In my days astronomy reached the market places. In these quite exceptional circumstances the steadfastness of one man could have shaken the world .... I betrayed my profession. A man who does what I have done cannot be tolerated in the ranks of science."

9

FOUNDATIONS OF A MARXIST
PHILOSOPHY OF MAN

We may now return to the general problem of the
need, task and place of a philosophy of man within the
general system of human thought. But we return en-
riched with certain considerations in the field of the
philosophy of man, which I have tried to indicate rather
than to finalise. We can, however, perhaps grasp the
problem differently now. It is now no longer a question
of whether man may be the legitimate subject of philosophy, but of the range and possible directions of such
philosophy.

What problems enter into the field of investigation of
a philosophy of man? And what are the lines of demarcation between this philosophy and the humanist sciences,
such as anthropology, sociology, individual and social
psychology? I have already indicated some of the problems; and I should say at once that, in my opinion, there
can be no rigid demarcation here between what is philosophical and what strictly pertains to one or other of
the empirical sciences. In general, a philosophy of man
differs from any of the special sciences of man by ap-
plying itself to its subject in a different manner. The
central axis of the philosophical investigation of man
is the definition of the essence of the individual's role
in his relations with society as a whole and with
other individuals within society. Around this central

axis revolve a wide range of problems concerning the destinies of individuals in their relations with the external world, and the social obligations and moral responsibilities of individuals.

So understood, the philosophy of man absorbs the problems of traditional ethics, creating a foundation for their analysis and solution. In my opinion, the demand for "a Marxist ethics" will not be realised until that ethics is developed in the spirit of a broadly understood philosophy of man.

This demand is often confused with the demand for some kind of Marxist code of morals, a substitute for the Ten Commandments. Such confusion is understandable. For what is more understandable than the illusion that the difficulties, including the moral difficulties, of a period of social transformation may be overcome by some kind of new moral code, and that it is only a matter of laying down the rules? However, it remains an illusion. For a Marxist should know, in the first place, that moral codes arise from life as specific reflections in human consiousness of existing social relations, and so cannot be composed or decreed at will. And in the second place, a Marxist should know that the traditional type of code was always formulated in the belief that moral standards were imposed on man somehow from outside, and because of that had a religious character even when they had an outwardly lay appearance. If it is agreed that man is the master of his own destiny, as the whole of modern knowledge demonstrates, and if the creative character of social and individual human practice is made the basis of our whole conception of the individual, society and history, then the idea of laying down moral standards from above in the traditional way becomes impossible.

Hence the philosophy of man includes ethics, but not the codification of morals. Historical materialism provides the theoretical basis for such a philosophy. It lays the basis for the social understanding of the individual, for setting the individual man against his social background, preserving his social essence, without losing what is personal in man.

Classical German idealist philosophy, by disclosing the active factor of human endeavour in man's relations with the external world, undoubtedly contributed to overcoming belief in the merely external determination of human behaviour. But so long as that thesis was tied to idealism it was impossible completely to overcome illusions of the external determination of human affairs. This task fell to the lot of Marxism, which shifted the problem of the active role of the individual onto a materialist foundation. Marxism thus created the premises for a materialist philosophy of man, which it further developed in its teachings on alienation and socialist humanism. But historical materialism is the premise for such a philosophy not the philosophy itself. The further development of a philosophy of man has today become a burning necessity for Marxism.

A philosophy of man can start off from two opposite principles:

1) That man's existence is the realisation of some superhuman conception or plan, external to man.

2) That man's existence is the creation of man himself—man makes himself, and the starting point of all considerations about man should be that he is autonomous.

These principles express respectively the religious conception that essence is prior to existence, and the lay conception that existence is prior and that what we call "essence" must be deduced from existence. The thesis of atheistic Existentialism, that existence is prior to essence, is a clear negation of the Tomist thesis that man's existence is participation in the essence and existence of God—or, to put it more simply, is decreed by Providence and not made what it is by the activity of man himself. In this general sense of opposition to the religious conception of the external determination of human destiny, every materialist, including the Marxist materialist, approves the Existentialist thesis. For the materialist also recognises human existence as the true point of departure for the investigation of human affairs. But the problem only begins where the Existentialist supposes it ends.

The whole findings of a philosophy of man depend on how one understands human existence.

In speaking of existence as contrasted to essence we refer to the real life of man, and not to the idea of what it should be. But if our interest lies in real human life, we may still approach the matter from two different aspects,

    1) from the aspect of men acting in society and on nature, that is, of the material life of man,

    2) from the aspect of the spiritual life of man, the spiritual activity of the human subject.

In the last analysis, the whole philosophy of man will depend on which of these aspects we select as fundamental for the interpretation of human existence. Merely to speak of "existence" does not prejudge whether we shall regard this existence from its subjective or its objective, material aspect. Marxism adopts the latter standpoint. But Existentialism cannot adopt it if it wishes to remain faithful to its own teachings.

To be an Existentialist it is not enough, as some believe, only to say that existence is prior to essence. As we have seen, materialism, from which Existentialism so energetically separates itself, says this too. In order to be an Existentialist it is necessary to say that the individual is "lonely", "condemned to freedom", and the rest of it. An Existentialist believes that the individual possesses absolute freedom of choice, and is himself alone and in isolation responsible for his choice and deeds. He must therefore renounce all determinism and historical necessity. And this imposes upon Existentialism a subjectivist conception of the individual and his existence. Existentialism is a closed subjectivist system: it cannot choose at will between different interpretations of existence, unless it is prepared to contradict its own teachings. Jean Hyppolite, who claims to be a supporter of Sartre's version of Existentialism, told us in Warsaw that Existentialism maintains "the unity of subjective and objective" in the real stream of events of human life. But Sartre's Existentialism implies a subjective interpretation of human existence, and Hyppolite is mistaken in thinking that Existentialism can adopt a realist interpretation, and survive—just as Sartre is mistaken in thinking it possible to patch together Marxism and Existentialism.

The problem of the creative historical role of the human individual has to be understood against this same background. Not only the individual's existence but his creative role, and his status in the world of things and people surrounding him, can be understood in two ways.

Understood in one way—in a realist way, from the aspect of the material life of man—man's creative possibilities, which are related to the nature of his freedom, are not unlimited. Man acts on the material world and, by transforming it, creates new conditions of his own existence. Man is the product of material conditions, of his natural and social environment, and at the same time shapes those conditions. "The educator must himself be educated," as Marx said: the conditions shaping man must in turn be shaped by him. But this does not signify that man can do whatever he likes. Man always confronts the real material world with its objective laws, and does not by his action annul those laws. His freedom does not consist in annulling necessity but in recognising and making use of it.

But there is another interpretation of human creativeness arising from the subjectivist interpretation of human existence. With this, the objective factors disappear, natural and social realities dissolve in the subject and his "creative activity". Man takes the place of God and, indeed, surpasses God—in as much as the latter created the material world and its laws only once, while man is supposed to be its creator in permanence.

Although Existentialism modestly pretends to be only a philosophy of man it nevertheless implies, as we now see, a complete idealist methaphysic.

We thus find ourselves again at the crossroads, which proves how differently a philosophy of man may be constructed by taking off from supposedly similar assumptions. Obviously, there is a connection between a philosophy of man and a general world outlook. A Marxist philosophy of man is explicitly based on materialism.

PART THREE

CONFLICTING HUMANISMS

10

THE SOCIALIST PERSPECTIVE

The present century will go down in history as the turning point in which was decided the victory of the new socialist social order on a world scale. It suffices to look back over the past half century to see with the naked eye—without being equipped with the instruments of scientific analysis—the tremendous social changes that have already taken place. Fifty years ago those who spoke of the necessity of socialist revolution were regarded either as utopian dreamers or dangerous criminals. Who at that time seriously thought, except the Marxists themselves, that the revolutionists, hounded and suppressed by the police, and mostly in gaol or in exile, would soon take power as leaders of a great working-class movement? And when the socialist revolution triumphed in 1917, who except the Marxists seriously believed that it could be consolidated and lay the foundations for the ultimate triumph of the new system on a world scale? Is not the distance travelled by the revolutionary labour movement in that period indeed fantastic? From scattered underground groups of revolutionaries it has become a powerful party guiding the state in countries that play an ever more decisive part in determining the course of world history. The road traversed has led from the poverty and hunger that accompanied the first beginnings of the revolution to the economic might of the socialist world; from cultural, scientific and technological backwardness to incontestable leadership in these fields.

It is the road from a single, isolated socialist state, encircled by capitalism, to a socialist world embracing more than a third of humanity, which in the epoch of the final dissolution of colonialism is acquiring a clear superiority over capitalism in the world relationship of forces. What a fantastic pace of development this has been!—from the first acts of the socialist revolution to today, when the powerfully united revolutionary movement confronts a new Holy Alliance, patched together and torn with sharper internal contradictions than ever its historical predecessor was.

These are striking, decisive facts. Is it not rather strange, therefore, that many of our contemporaries are blind to them? Not so strange, perhaps, for bigoted opponents of socialism, whose social position distorts their view of events and leads them to wishful thinking— though even some of our opponents are beginning to appreciate the world situation, and to strike a Cassandra note in speaking of it. But what of those who have now parted company with the revolutionary movement but are still subjectively connected with it?

That some claim to be disillusioned, and a few of them are very noisy about it, cannot be explained simply from the shock sustained from the revelation of the so-called "cult of the individual" in the Soviet Union. In my opinion something deeper is involved. The causes of this reaction have been latent among many people for a long time, and were only released by the shocks of recent years. It is necessary to analyse these causes if only for the purpose of therapy—or perhaps rather auto-therapy; since only by taking proper account of causes is it possible to overcome their effects.

Historical analogies are shifty and deceptive instruments of historical analysis, for a true picture of historical events always requires comprehension of the specific peculiarities of a specific set of conditions. Yet within definite limits, and with judicious use, historical analogy may be a valuable instrument for confirming the well known truth that history is "the teacher of life". It has been a traditional mistake, in my opinion, to believe that analyses of the labour movement and of socialism do not allow for any historical comparisons and analogies, but deal with entirely new and in every respect specific phenomena. The labour movement and socialism are indeed new phenomena of history, different in kind from anything that has gone before. But to make this difference absolute is harmful to research and inquiry.

Let us consider the atmosphere of public opinion in past periods of struggle for the transition from new social ideals to their realisation. Clearly, any mechanical, shallow analogy between the Cromwellian or Jacobin revolutions and the October Revolution would be absurd, if only because entirely different social forces made them under entirely different conditions. The socialist revolution is historically a new and unique event. But it does not follow that there cannot exist any kind of general pattern in the course of revolutions, which may appear in such otherwise different social phenomena as the French and Russian revolutions.

Various historians, some of them very able ones, have studied the influence on the course of the French Revolution of the ideas which preceded it. Less studied have been the questions of how society, and particularly its intellectual circles, accepted the post-revolutionary reality, and how the ideas which prepared the ground for the revolution corresponded with their realisation in life.

What we do know justifies the conclusion that great confusion reigned, especially in intellectual circles, and that conflicting reactions took place. The plebian elements soon discovered that "Liberty, equality and fraternity" meant different things for different people; and their discontent with the way the ideas of the revolution were being translated into life found expression in the Babeuf movement. Others, adherents of bourgeois ideology, also experienced a shock of disillusionment, for different reasons: they were scared when they saw their own cherished ideals bring realised. Goethe was a typical example. In short, dissatisfaction arose not only because to the revolutionary chariot were harnessed, as in the fable, a crab, a pike and a swan; not only because different forces diverged, which were for a time united in the struggle against a common enemy. An important role was evidently played by the shock typically engendered by the transition from proclaimed ideals to their realisation. It is precisely here that a general pattern may be discerned, which extends beyond the framework of bourgeois revolutions and, as it seems to me, appears also in socialist revolutions.

One effect of the complex character of social reality is that general ideas work out differently, when it comes to their realisation, from what was intended when they were originally promulgated. And the intervention of the time factor also results in divergences from original purposes.

The desire to shorten historical perspectives is characteristic of all revolutionary movements. This explains the impatience of reformers, among other things. Even Marx did not escape it: his forecasts in *The Communist Manifesto* were justified some seventy years later than he expected. William Morris described the socialist revolution as commencing in Britain in 1952, and some of his friends thought him pessimistic in putting it off so long. The difference in time alone means that events turn out differently from what was originally anticipated, since with the passage of time they develop under changed conditions.

However, not only the desire to shorten historical perspectives is involved here, but also the simplification of the assumed structure of reality. This is a basic element in the generation later on of conflicts in the course of realising given ideals.

This is, perhaps, a mainly psychological problem. But social psychology is an integral part of sociology. People who are fighting against a given system because of the evils associated with it are naturally inclined to wish for a social order which would be the absolute negation of all those evils. If one fights against the exploitation of man by man, one has in view the ideal of a society without exploitation. If one fights against a system that puts a premium on selfishness, one fights for a system in which true altruism and brotherhood will be realised. If one fights against a system which strangles the development of culture and the arts, one aspires to a system which will be a model of freedom and progress in these fields. In this way one builds up a set of values which show what is wrong with things as they are; and then what one is fighting against is the basis for the image of what one is fighting for.

Such an approach is not only normal and understandable, it is necessary. Assurance of the effectiveness of the struggle against existing evil helps to create the new reality.

For the modern labour movement, guided by the Marxist science of society, the whole complex process of negations and affirmations rests on the scientific analysis of capitalism and of the new social forces which assure the possibility of constructing a socialist system. The fantastic and utopian element in the definition of a social goal is eliminated for the first time in history. It is eliminated by the scientific analysis of the root causes of social evil and of the way to correct it. This is the basis for the claim of socialism to be a science. And from this it follows that the image of the future society to be created by the modern working-class movement is of a fundamentally different nature from that engendered by previous revolutionary movements. But the revolutionary socialist movement has at least this element in common with previous movements, that it cherishes an ideal, an ideal model of the future society—although this ideal is of a different origin. And precisely here is latent the danger of confusing dissimilar things—ideals with practical life, a projected image with actually existing realities.

Of course, every proficient Marxist—indeed, every reasonable person—knows that socialism cannot be built in a moment, that it is impossible by a single revolutionary decree to abolish all remnants of the past, that a new system can be perfected only by a long process of struggle, and that it is in any case impossible, so long as human beings remain of flesh and blood, to create a utopia completely free from any human conflicts and contradictions. All this is clear in theory, and was long ago settled for every Marxist.

However, the road from theory to practice is always hard and long. Each of us shaped his socialist convictions by picturing to himself an ideal future. Some who are older did so in gaols, in underground struggle, in the daily and often discouraging fight against capitalism; and the youth, in the romantic period of the first post-revolutionary years. We may be fully aware that social processes are long and complicated; but the consciousness that socialism "is here", that the threshold of the revolution has already been crossed, stirs the imagination and makes it intolerable if the promises of socialism are delayed in realisation. One may theorise as much as one likes, but people do rebel when they see signs, and not just sporadic ones, of injustice, pilfering, race hatred, obscurantism, egotism. One may say, "Such things are inevitable for a time"; but the question still arises: "And is this socialism?" One may be told that these evils were not created by socialism, but carried over from the old society; but the reply comes pat: "It was bad then too, but no one called it socialism."

It is here, in my opinion, that many of the reasons for our recent difficulties and crisis lie concealed. These difficulties stem from the gap between ideals and practical reality, values and the process of realising them, rational knowledge and spontaneous emotion, the patience of the theoretician and the impatience of the person who has to live his life in the given society.

Is there any justification for the inner revolt of people who feel more strongly about evils in a socialist society than in the previous society? Yes and no. Yes, if it is a question of feeling the need to oppose evil. Forbearance towards evil and reconciliation with it is itself an evil, which no sociological explanation of the reasons for delay and the complicated character of the transformation of social consciousness can excuse. Of course, socialism is built by people brought up under capitalism and carrying its stigma. But the conditions under which these same people are now acting are different. As a social system, socialism creates the conditions for overcoming the personal traits and attitudes produced by capitalism. This is why the protest against social evil should be stronger, and the struggle against it more determined, under socialism. Resentment against evil in socialist society is a truly sacred resentment.

But we must still understand that resentment alone is not enough to effect a change in social relations and people's consciousness. The necessary conditions must be created, and this does take time. If this were understood, the protest against evil would not create crises and despair, but the conviction of the need to struggle against evils the origins and persistence of which we understand. It is a mistake not to see socialism as a historical process, just as it is wrong to deduce from the evils we see any practical conclusions except the need and the manner of fighting against them. Only one concrete condition can be demanded for the realisation of the socialist ideal: to combat social evils intelligently and in an organised manner. They cannot be abolished by decree.

Evidently, then, it is no easy thing to distinguish what

should be from what actually is at a given stage of development. The ability or inability to master this art of distinction had a strong influence on the various expressions of the ideological crisis which arose in Poland in 1956. One need only to have followed attentively the various discussions which took place among us of recent years in politics, morality and philosophy, to realise the depth of misunderstanding and crisis generated by the confusion of absolute values, functioning as a system of ideals, with practical reality, always characterised by relative, socially conditioned values which can be appreciated only in their true historical prespective.

Observation of social reality clarifies still another, and no less important, aspect of our problem: the tendency to lose the socialist perspective and abandon ideals in the jungle of daily trifles amongst which one lives. This is a serious and ever present danger. For, on the one hand, to see the world only in comparison with ideal patterns, to lose the sense of reality and fail to understand the dynamics of real life, threatens a breakdown in practice occasioned by disappointment with real life. On the other hand, to be immersed in daily affairs and in narrow practicalism leads to loss of perspective, to forgetting the goal, and hence again to a breakdown in practice. The starting points are different, the outcome is the same. One sees only the statics of social life and not the dynamics.

It is usual for some people to adjust their ideology to this second sin also, and to try to pass it off as a virtue. These are disciples of their own brand of pragmatism. Our daily life is often none too easy, with the inherited a-morality, muddleheadedness and obscurantism, the selfishness, egotism and suspicious attitude to fellow citizens carried over from our former social life, with our own traditional indolence, which has not yet been lost, with the bad attitude to work. How often does it appear to our pragmatists that we who aspire to an ideal are engaged in the labour of Sisyphus—that most terrible of the punishments imposed by the gods of antiquity! It is then that they lose heart. It is then that their famous practicality comes to an end, and they turn out to be ordinary cynics.

Noone in our country is condemned to the labour of Sisyphus. But thousands carry on courageously, even in face of the greatest difficulties and hazards, when they acquire a perspective in which the present, with all its shortcomings, is understood in its historical sense. In its result, pragmatism is a philosophy good only for cynics and spiritual bankrupts. Active life, social struggle, all progressive action and struggle, require a perspective and the consciousness of the goal towards which men are labouring. The need for such an ideology was ruthlessly and ignorantly scorned by some circles in our country for a certain period. This attitude threatened inevitable bankruptcy. The goal and perspective must be kept always in view, in order not to lose hope, not to break down under the pressure of daily cares and hardships. It is also necessary in order not to get bogged down in narrow practicality and taking a fancy to easy ways of conducting oneself, which are perhaps natural but certainly cannot be considered a virtue.

From this standpoint, knowledge of the principles of socialist humanism is of the greatest importance for the builders of socialism.

II

THE APPEAL OF SOCIALIST HUMANISM

Socialist humanism defines the essential social content of the idea of socialism. Socialism can be defined in various ways, by emphasising one or another of its aspects or purposes. But all are subordinate to the central aim of the all-sided development of man. Man is the starting point and final aim of socialism, and it is man's purposive activity that brings it into being. Humanism is the outlook which sees the all-sided development of the human individual as the goal of human activity. Socialist as distinct from other kinds of humanism links the realisation of this goal with the specific social and economic aims of socialism. Marxism took its point of departure from humanism, and in theory and practice its concern has been with human affairs.

Recent history has been the history of the competition between two systems, socialism and capitalism. An objective view of the record of this competition, an objective examination of the facts, makes evident the attractive force of the ideas of Communism which, in recent decades, have induced such a basic and decisive shift in social forces.

People who struggle against the capitalists in the name of socialism, and by dint of the greatest sacrifices in the cause of socialism abolish capitalism in a revolutionary way, do so by their own free choice. Such a choice in favour of socialism has been made by tens of millions of people throughout the world. It is an undeniable fact that additional hundreds of millions, particularly in Asia and Latin America, but also in Europe, are ready to make the same choice today and are prevented only by main force. This plebiscite of the masses attests to the final collapse of capitalism.

What guides people in making such a choice? What appeals to their minds and hearts? What is it that unites in the choice of socialism the Russian worker, the Italian peasant, the Chinese intellectual, the villager of Laos, the Cuban peasant and the many, many others engaged in a life and death struggle against capitalism? Perhaps it is what we call humanism, although most often people do not use this learned term.

Despite enemy propaganda, despite the grievous errors committed in the course of its realisation, the power of attraction of socialism lies primarily in the fact that people who are oppressed and exploited see in socialism the answer to their problems, their hope of a better life. People come to socialism by different roads. With some it is material need, with others national oppression, with still others moral revulsion against the existing system. But all are united by the conviction that socialism is the remedy for the social evils they are combatting, that socialism can deliver them from those evils and create better conditions of human life. Socialism does not appeal to people because of its wealth and power, for it had a strong attraction when it was still poor and weak, and some capitalist countries are richer than any socialist countries even today. Nor does it appeal to the majority by the intellectual content and superiority of its philosophical and economic doctrines. But all who chose socialism, even those not yet able to explain what they understand by the word, are attracted by its humanist content. This is something that both opponents of socialism and socialists absorbed in narrow practicality often fail to appreciate.

I have read with great satisfaction and personal pleasure

a number of writings by Western specialists on the subject of Communism, variations on the worn-out theme that "Communist ideology is dead". I say "worn-out", because the authors must explain why the dead ideas continue to appeal and even to make progress. Particularly in the United States this manner of writing has become not only usual but highly subsidised. And so I read this kind of stuff with genuine satisfaction, because it characterises the opponent and shows what he is like and how much he knows. I am persuaded that it is an advantage to have a badly informed and stupid opponent. What we may read in these writings confirms the opinion that neither the extent of their information nor the depth of their analysis is at all impressive.

The matter is very simple in the case of the American writers. Their writing is an expression of the wishful thinking which is so characteristic of political life in the United States. They simply refuse to recognise unpleasant facts. The existence of Communist ideology and its influence over people is an unpleasant fact, to them—and so they say it is dead. But Americans, of all people, should know that you cannot "conceal America". They should ask themselves why this dead ideology is dealing such heavy blows against the supposedly live ideology which they subsidise, not only in distant Asia but rather close at hand in Latin America. Are not the Americans themselves raising the alarm about the "infiltration" of Communist ideas, and complaining that the Communists are seducing innocent folk from their proper allegiance? Assuming that that is so, the question is why these folk are so easily led astray by the ideas of Communism, while the Americans, for all their efforts, have their work cut out convincing them of the life-giving qualities of the American way of life.

The trump card of anti-Marxist and anti-Communist propaganda has been the question of the rights of the individual under socialism, the question of democracy.

Our opponents labour hard to prove that they have a democracy and we a dictatorship, that the rights of the individual are respected in their countries and not in ours. This is an argument that really does appeal to many people, and can for a time effectively frighten them away from socialism. In so far as it is effective, our own mistakes must contribute to that effect; and so I would like to devote some attention to this question.

We have sometimes, as I have said, sadly neglected the philosophical problems connected with the individual and his affairs. We can explain but not excuse this neglect. And it was bound to create a misunderstanding of our position on the question of the individual, which could be exploited by enemy propaganda. For years, too, we have often deliberately used language which cannot easily be understood by ordinary people; and this fact as well has been taken advantage of by our opponents. Without already possessing a deep knowledge of theory it is not easy to grasp that we are speaking of "the highest form of democracy" whenever we speak of "the dictatorship of the proletariat", and that this is no contradiction. It is one thing to use a scientific terminology, quite another to make it comprehensible. Finally, we have to admit and explain those episodes in the history of socialist construction which we have baptised by the name "mistakes and distortions"; but we cannot justify them, and should not try to. This, too, has been used against us by enemy propaganda.

How can we counteract misunderstandings which are so harmful to the dissemination of socialist ideas? First of all, by means of practice. This is the most effective and convincing argument. And this is why, although our opponents zealously exploit the field of investigation neglected by us and claim a monopoly of humanism, those to whom they address themselves still remain in some doubt as to who actually represents humanism. For them it is a question that is decided by people's practice.

This is why the toiling masses of Latin America or Southeast Asia have spontaneously embraced Communism, while all the Existentialisms and Personalisms remain for them esoteric doctrines.

But while the most important thing is whether the movement and its ideology are in practice humanist, the mere fact is not enough and people must be convinced of it. This is all the more necessary because the enemy tries hard to conceal and falsify the fact, and to represent our theory and practice as anti-humanist while himself flying the false colours of humanism.

This question has also an internal aspect for us. As stated in the last chapter, narrow practicalism is a danger to the building of socialism. It is a danger not only because preoccupation with current daily affairs brings a loss of perspective. It is a danger, above all, because whenever any individual right may be infringed because of the practical exigencies of some particular political situation, this infringement may come to be regarded as quite normal and may be perpetuated.

In such a situation is concealed, in embryo, the danger of violating the fundamental principle of socialism — socialist humanism. What we in our peculiar language call "mistakes and distortions" are, of course, always associated with the activities of some individual. But their roots go deep into the social political soil. There are no absolute guarantees against "distortions" of this kind. But that does not mean that it is not possible to take measures to prevent them. One way of conducting this struggle is to arm society ideologically, particularly those whose positions expose them most to the temptation of perpetrating such distortions. To acquaint society with the nature of distortions and their significance is an effective though not an absolute way of combatting violations of socialist humanism.

The wide dissemination of the principles of socialist humanism has therefore not only a propaganda but, above all, an educational value.

12

SOCIALIST HUMANISM
AND ITS FORERUNNERS

It is necessary to emphasise and give priority to what is historically new in the social practice and ideology of Marxism. But that is only a part of the truth. It is also true that Marxism, in its social and ideological content, is a continuation of many old ideas and currents of thought. Here we may repeat with King Solomon that "there is nothing new under the sun", and at the same time maintain with Heraclitus that "you cannot step into the same river twice".

Socialist humanism is simultaneously a new and specific doctrine, possible only within a new social context, and an old general trend with a long tradition. The more we underline what is new in it, the more must we stress its tradition. And we must do this because, amongst other things, it adds splendour and social weight to the new humanism. To divorce ourselves from tradition would impoverish our ideas and weaken their social influence—despite the opinion of the defenders of the "absolute" revolutionary newness of Marxism. It was Lenin who wrote: "The genius of Marx consists precisely in the fact that he furnished answers to questions the foremost minds of mankind had already raised. His teachings arose as the direct and immediate continuation of the teachings of the greatest representatives of philosophy, political economy and socialism."

Socialist humanism is not new in any absolute sense. It is as old as the palpitation of the human heart at the sight of other people's unhappiness, as the protest against the sufferings of the oppressed and exploited, as the love of near ones, as the ideals of happiness and equality. Socialism humanism answers in a new way the question of how it is possible to attain the goal of human wellbeing; what should be attained was known long ago by the best minds of mankind, although they often spoke in a language now strange to us and from the point of view of religious movements and religious beliefs. True, general maxims which have survived for hundreds and thousands of years take on new content under new social conditions. Yet the humanist content of the commandment "love thy neighbour as thyself" has survived for two thousand years. Absolute morality and absolute commandments are nonsense from the standpoint of social science. But it is a scientific truth that there are human relationships which manifest themselves in every form of social life, and are reflected in humanist ideas, regardless of differences in social context and social outlook.

Socialist humanism expresses the essential content of the modern Communist movement, which fights for the best possible social conditions, for the individual's happiness, for the best conditions for the development of the human personality by the abolition of such obstacles to it as material want and economic, national, racial and cultural inequality. The Communist movement fights for these aims under new conditions and in a new way. But the aims were formulated long ago. People long ago dreamed of fulfilling humanist ideals in human life—they fought throughout the ages and perished in struggles for them. Without those struggles our humanism would not be what it is today. The greatest philosophers, political leaders and revolutionaries were the protagonists of humanism. They belong to our history and our tradition, including prophets and religious leaders later canonised and worshipped even today like gods. Their teachings are noble, regardless of their form, and belong within the great line of development of the ideas of humanism from which we also stem. Of course, we can distinguish closer and more distant relations among them, we can distinguish between lines of legitimate descent and those of illegitimate kinship. But none of them are complete strangers to us, and we should not surrender any of them to the family tree of our opponents.

In so strongly emphasising the bond between socialist humanism and its forerunners it is necessary at the same time to understand its specific nature, its uniqueness, which is of decisive importance for investigating its character and its prospects of realisation.

All general definitions of humanism commit the sin of improper abstraction, since they ignore concrete historical conditions. A proper estimation of a given school of humanism, and in particular a choice between its contemporary varieties, requires social analysis, that is, considerations of concrete conditions of time and place.

Every epoch has had its own type of humanism. All the reform and revolutionary movements of a given period, directed against the existing forms of oppression and exploitation, inequality and social injustice, are in the final analysis reducible to humanism. In this sense we can speak of ancient humanism, of the humanism of early Christianity, of the Renaissance, the Reformation, the Englightenment and Utopian Socialism. Each type of humanism may in this sense be evaluated historically from the standpoint of a given period. Such evaluation would generally be positive, but only as a historical assessment. The matter is different, however, when we are faced with the task of judging between different contemporary currents of humanism and making a choice between them—when, for instance, socialist humanism clashes with the social actuality of the various brands of bourgeois humanism.

Here it is a question of choice, and the criteria of choice are therefore of decisive importance. Two considerations come to the fore: (1) which of the competing humanisms is most radical, in the sense of giving the maximum consideration to the vital questions of the development of the individual; (2) which is most realistic, most practical for the realisation of the ideals put forward as the goal of social action.

Socialist humanism is distinguished from other varieties by the nature of the social movement which conceives it, the social force which promotes it, and the historical conditions which make the emancipation of the working class the condition for the emancipation of all humanity. Thus socialist humanism is distinguished by its concrete content. An analysis of differences between socialist and other humanism may be made from different angles, but regardless of the point of departure it will return in one way or another to the above considerations. It is with this in mind that I say that the main distinguishing feature of socialist humanism is that it is a *militant* humanism.

In a certain sense, every type of humanism contains an element of struggle. Whether humanism bases itself on moral sentiments (utopian), religious commandments (religious), or the perfectibility of human nature (enlightenment), fights to win people. But socialist humanism understands in its own way the nature of the struggle to realise its ideals. For the first time in history, socialist humanism is not derived from religious commandments or from innate human nature, but from a scientific theory of social development, in which the ideals of humanism are linked with the interests of definite social classes, and from which is derived the road towards the realisation of the ideals and the social forces to be mobilised for that purpose. Humanist ideals are thus brought down from the clouds of moral-utopian abstraction to the firm ground of social political struggle. Ideals do not by that stop being ideals, but they stop being utopias. They become the realistic aim of political struggle.

Socialist humanism is therefore the reverse of abstract and moralistic humanism, owing to its concrete and militant nature. By its concreteness I mean, first, that socialist humanism is concerned, not with man in the abstract, but with men in their actual social and historical conditions, and with the actual needs and possibilities of development arising from those conditions. And I mean second, that socialist humanism is not concerned with absolute but with relative values and standards of conduct, which flow from the dialectics of real life situations, of the struggle to realise our ideals. Much may be said under these two headings. But here I will limit myself to speaking of the dialectical phenomena which flow from the militant character of socialist humanism.

There is a dialectic of love and hate in human life, and humanism, generally considered, rests on the "love thy neighbour" precept. Its aim is "everything for the sake of man", for the full and unhindered development of the individual. Is "love thy neighbour", then, an absolute commandment? To be a humanist must one adopt the attitude of consistent Christians or of Ghandi, and re-nounce all physical force in favour of exclusively moral struggle by turning the other cheek? Our answer is, no.

The aim of militant humanism is the development of the individual and the creation of the best possible conditions for his happiness. In this it does not differ from other humanisms. But militant humanism not only declares such an aim, but fights for it. In real life we are confronted, not with man in general, but with people who defend definite interests and are correspondingly motivated and organised. The humanist ideal which promotes the interest of some—the exploited and oppressed—goes against the interest of others—the exploiters and oppressors. What is more, in real life the latter are bound to oppose with all their strength the realisation of the humanist ideal, and to try to put an end to the ideology which advocates it. The fact that in modern capitalist society you have to fight for humanist goals is not something invented, since the struggle *against* the aims of humanism is a basic fact and characteristic trait of modern capitalism. Socialist humanism is concerned with the realisation of humanist aims under the concrete conditions of modern society divided by class struggles. It hence demands not only love for the people, but hatred of their enemies. Its attitude was expressed long ago in the words of James Connolly:

> *"Then comrades, sing a rebel song,*
> *A song of love and hate,*
> *Of love unto the lowly*
> *And of hatred to the great."*

Socialist humanism rejects absolute values and standards, for they are false and do not lead towards the goal. On the contrary, they block the road to it, since real life situations are conflicting situations. Hatred for the sake of love is not a paradox, but a consequence of the realities of a situation in which the realisation of humanist ideals is impossible without struggle against the advocates and practitioners of anti-humanism. Those who love people must hate the opponents of the people's wellfare. To be a humanist does not mean to love people in general, to advocate abstract pacifism, to reject all physical struggle. To be a humanist today, when the realisation of humanist ideals is no longer a utopia, is to be a fighter. And he who fights well must hate well. It is hence possible and necessary in the name of love of one's neightbour to hate those who oppress him, and to fight for human brotherhood against those who deny brotherhood.

The dialectics of freedom and its limitation also follows from the basic fact of the class struggle in modern society.

The goal of socialist humanism is the all-sided development of the individual, and hence his freedom. But is freedom something absolute? No, just as the demand for absolute love is a mockery in conditions of struggle, so is the demand for absolute freedom. As long as there are enemies of freedom, as long as they can fight effectively, so long will it be necessary to strive to limit their freedom. How and to what degree this becomes necessary depends on the conditions and character of the struggle.

Does this not create a grave danger of abuses? And would it not therefore be better to abjure any kind of limitation on freedom whatsoever? Yes, there is a danger—but unlimited freedom for the enemies of freedom is a danger of an altogether different order: it spells certain disaster for freedom. This is why socialist humanism advocates limiting freedom as much as is necessary for the sake of freedom.

The dialectics of democracy and dictatorship is another expression of the conflicts latent in our social structure. Marxism holds that full democracy can be attained only by means of a dictatorship exercised against the enemies of democracy, and regards the dictatorship of the proletariat as a higher form of democracy in comparison with bourgeois democracy.

These questions of freedom and its limitation, of democracy and dictatorship, are closely connected and constitute the most difficult problem of socialist humanism. The next chapter will be devoted to them.

13

THE FREEDOM OF THE INDIVIDUAL

Freedom is as vital for the development of human personality as is the satisfaction of material needs. Both are equally essential. Yet such is the dialectic of human freedom that every consideration of it has to acknowledge the necessity of limiting it in one way or another.

When we speak of the freedom of the individual we are speaking of the rights of the individual in society—for there is no individual outside society. The moment this truth is recognised any illusions about absolute freedom are dispersed, and the problem opens up of determining the permissible limits of restriction of freedom, and of fixing the demarcation line between the condition we are ready to accept as one of freedom and that to which we must deny this splendid quality.

The freedom of one individual is limited by that of others. So much is self-evident, and is universally recognised. But the problem of freedom involves more than that—at least, if we relate it to man as a social being and not to imaginary "abstract man". For every individual is a component part of some social class, sharing its interests and claiming its rights. Hence it is not merely that the freedom of one individual is limited by that of others, but that there is conflict between the freedoms of different social classes.

It is obvious that freedom cannot be confused with doing whatever you like. But once we try to determine precisely where freedom ends and anarchy begins, the illusory simplicity and clarity of the above statement vanishes, especially when we treat the individual's affairs in their real context—as connected with some class and interwoven with class interests.

Let us consider, for example, the freedom of a serf and a lord under feudalism, and of a factory worker and a factory owner under capitalism. People generally express no doubts at all today about the first case. Of course the desires for freedom of the serf tied to the soil and of the lord living on his labour are mutually contradictory, and that contradiction was one of the main motive forces of the peasant revolts in the middle ages. And to the unprejudiced investigator, the conflicting desires for freedom, and the associated conceptions of freedom, of the factory worker and factory owner under capitalism appear equally contradictory. What, then, is individual freedom, and in what consists its violation? How shall we judge the conflict between freedom to exploit and freedom from exploitation? This depends on one's system of values and conception of freedom, which in turn hinge upon one's affiliation to a given class and identification with its dominant interests.

The freedom of one class is restricted or even destroyed by the freedom of another, and so they have different conceptions of freedom. The state apparatus now becomes involved in the conflict. Its function is to guard and serve those conceptions of freedom which follow from the interests of the dominant classes. This is the function of political or state power in even the most democratic states, so long as society is divided into antagonistic classes.

In antiquity, democracy embraced only the freemen. As regards the slaves—if we disregard the conflicts between free citizens—the ancient state was a dictatorship which deprived them of every vestige of freedom. Democracy in the middle ages, in so far as it existed at all, was also limited to certain classes—the nobility or the burghers of city republics. All who did not belong to the privileged groups were ruled by dictatorship. The bourgeoisie introduced formal equality of citizens before the law, but it in fact maintained an economic inequality from which diverse social conflicts resulted. Bourgeois democracy is also limited and is directed against definite sections of society—either openly by providing special benefits to the privileged classes, or covertly by making use of the factual power of wealth.

Points of detail may be disputed, but no candid investigator of political relations can question either the conflicting nature of freedom in class society or the part played by the state in this conflict. It by no means follows that there is no difference between a democratic regime and an out-and-out dictatorship, or that the degree of democracy is of no consequence. Quite the contrary. But it does follow that, being a class institution, democracy is always limited, and that, as the embodiment of the attitude to freedom of some social class, every democracy is a dictatorship in relation to some other class.

Such is the meaning of the Marxist contention that every democracy is a form of class dictatorship. There is a close connection between the fact that individual freedom in a class society is limited by the dominant class relations—the freedom of different individuals belonging to different classes exists only within these relations—and the circumstance that democracy in such a society is also limited by these class relations and always has its dictatorial side. To say that every democracy is at the same time a dictatorship is to maintain that democracy is a form of power, of domination; and that in a class society power is always used to rule and dominate over some in the interests of others.

What conclusion can be drawn from this? The fullest extension of individual freedom can be effected only by the final elimination of class society, together with the conflicting interests and attitudes to freedom associated with it, thereby eliminating democracy as a form of domination of some over others. This Marxist conclusion is of the greatest significance for humanism, the aim of which is the maximum extension of the individual's freedom as the means to the fullest development of his personality.

The Marxist conception of communist society is one in which, as I have said, the cardinal ideals of humanism are realised, while those ideals in turn stem from the image of the future society. For this is a vision of a society which has overcome every kind of alienation in social life—I use this word unwillingly, because it is capable of many meanings; but here I mean primarily the alienation represented by the state as a power dominating over man, and the alienation of the products of labour, which as products of man come to dominate over him. And the ending of alienation creates hitherto unknown and vast possibilities for the development of the individual.

The individual, then, can acquire maximum freedom only under the following conditions:

1) in a classless society in which the private ownership of means of production is abolished and with it the contradictory freedoms of conflicting classes;

2) when, as a consequence, the state as a political instrument based on force withers away;

3) when democracy, therefore, in its traditional meaning, also withers away.

But this will not create the absolute freedom demanded by anarchists. For there will operate even then certain laws of social life limiting the voluntary conduct of the individual. Such limitations, flowing from the needs of human co-operation, will be universally obligatory, whereas the limitations of freedom stemming from the conflicts between exploiters and exploited, rulers and ruled, will disappear. Freedom will be extended in this manner within limits determined by social necessity, that is, by the necessary requirements of the organisation of social life.

Such is the general outline of the conditions necessary to realise the maximum freedom of the individual, the conditions affording him the fullest possibilities of benefiting from this freedom. But it is necessary not only to possess the possibilities but also the ability to benefit from them. The abolition of every antithesis between mental and manual labour, between town and countryside, the social emancipation of women, and so on—all these things must be brought about in order that under the new system every individual will have the ability to develop his personality fully and a new type of man will take shape. These are very important matters which require separate consideration. I wished only to mention them here, in order not to oversimplify the Marxist vision of the future society.

Of course, this is still only a vision. But there can be no doubt—and not even the most bitter enemies of Communism can reasonably deny it—that it is a deeply humanist vision. Its revolutionary character consists not only in its thorough-going conception of freedom, but in the fact that it is based on a scientific analysis of social life and on realistic expectations of the outcome of concrete struggle by definite social forces. These are the elements which determine the superiority of socialist humanism over all its competitors.

I now want to go back to the consideration of the Marxist conception of the dictatorship of the proletariat as the form of the state in the period of transition from capitalism to socialism.

The partial liquidation of privileges of birth and the introduction of the formal principle of equality of citizens before the law are historical achievements of the bourgeois state. Socialism represents a new achievement in the realisation of equality since, besides finally eliminating privileges of birth, it creates for all members of society the privileges accruing from the social ownership of the means of production. It thereby transforms formal into actual equality. This makes it possible in the course of further development to abolish inequalities flowing from the differences between mental and manual labour, between town and countryside, and so on, of which I spoke above. Indeed, the abolition of the privileges resulting from private property is the foundation of all social progress.

Hence the proletarian revolution raises democracy to a new and higher level. By changing the foundations of equality, by eliminating exploitation of man by man and thereby abolishing the traditional classes, it creates a new situation in the realm of freedom.

Nevertheless Marxist socialism calls the state of the transition period "the dictatorship of the proletariat". Is it correct and consistent to do so?

Of course, the name does not in any way change the fact that the dictatorship of the proletariat is the state of socialist democracy. The use of a name emphasising the dictatorial and not the democratic side of the new state has a historical justification. The Communist movement wanted sharply to distinguish its own from the bourgeois-liberal and social-democratic conceptions of the state. The terminology came into use in controversies concerning the nature of the class struggle under capitalism and of the socialist revolution.

It would perhaps seem like stating the obvious here to emphasise the dictatorial function of socialist democracy in view of the conflicts already mentioned between different conceptions of freedom and the role of the state in these conflicts. The state is always a class instrument. This applies both to the state which stands guard over the freedom of the capitalist class and to the state which, after the dispossession of the capitalists, protects the freedom of the working masses. In every post-revolutionary period the state is at one and the same time a dictatorship in relation to the overthrown classes—which threaten to restore their rule and to call in foreign intervention—and a new and higher form of democracy for those who overthrew them. The Jacobin state was a bloody dictatorship in relation to the aristocracy; but few would doubt today that it introduced a new and higher type of democracy. It is the latter fact which determines the character of that state, and not the revolutionary terror. Perhaps the terror exceeded the bounds necessary to defeat the counter-revolution. But who knows and who today can maintain with complete certainty that that was so?

A decisive feature of the democracy of the proletarian state is that, besides abolishing privileges based on property and their political effects it introduces a new type of people's power which develops new modes of social practice leading to the emergence of higher forms of social life.

There is ample proof of this in the daily life of the socialist states, in the dynamic of their development. Those who do not see this evidence or who stubbornly deny it simply do not want to see, or else are resorting to wishful thinking to conceal from themselves their own collapse.

Like other forms of democracy, socialist democracy does not refrain from the use of force. As a form of state power, socialist democracy is the dictatorship of some classes directed against other classes. It cannot be otherwise. But there is a danger latent in this fact, which can grow in magnitude in the period following the revolution, when the dictatorial side of the state power needs to be exerted most strongly. This is the danger of confusing means and ends, and of perpetuating exceptional measures when they are no longer justified by the objective situation, simply because it is easier to govern by means of force than by persuasion.

The danger here consists of alienating the functions of force. As I said above, I do not like the word "alienation" because it has many meanings and is historically weighted. Perhaps this is why Marx stopped using this term in his later writings. But it seems to fit the present case very well. For what happens here is that one of man's creations becomes alienated from him, becomes autonomous and begins to dominate over man, and means are transformed into the end itself.

The danger of such alienation of the functions and apparatus of force was exemplified in the French Revolution, and again in the so-called period of mistakes and distortions in our own revolution. It is a thing close to us, and very painful.

Are any absolute guarantees possible against succumbing to such a danger? In my opinion, there can be no absolute guarantees in politics. This is why those who at one time demanded "institutional guarantees" for socialism in our country, betraying thereby their desire for the parliamentary system to be introduced, were deeply mistaken. The frustration they are now experiencing can be ascribed only to their lack of political insight. I am not in principle opposed to the parliamentary system, nor in general to institutionalising socialist democracy. I am only concerned with recognising the historically conditioned character of particular institutions, as well as their limited value as guarantes against violations of democracy, against some organs of state power—such as the security services—becoming a law unto themselves, and so on. No institution and no "institutional guarantees" can stand up under the pressure of the needs of life and of politics. The bourgeoisie sweeps parliament itself, together with all the institutional guarantees, off the map, even in countries of old parliamentary tradition, as soon as it appears that this form of rule no longer ensures its domination. Italy, Weimar Germany and, later, France under de Gaulle all testify to this. There is no reason to doubt that the working class dictatorship would not hesitate to resort to drastic measures in case of need. But the crux of the matter is that the apparatus of force appears in the socialist system only as a temporary necessity in the transition period; the necessity of defending the socialist order overshadows all other considerations and so-called guarantees. No Communist denies this necessity; he only limits himself to demanding that it should not be abused. This is why the education of society in the spirit of socialist humanism, to the understanding of Communism's goal of human freedom, should play the foremost role in controlling the apparatus of force.

More than one reader may now be smiling sceptically. Can any educational measures help where even institutional guarantees are of no avail? But I think there is no ground for scepticism here.

The sceptics would be right if education in the spirit of socialist humanism were considered as the *only* means for securing immediate results. This would, of course, be a naive supposition. But to stress the role of social education along with all other institutional measures is undoubtedly realistic.

In speaking of the educational functions of socialist humanism I have in mind the systematic propagation of its ideas by the schools, in literature, in meetings and lectures, as well as their dissemination by appropriate administrative activity. The latter includes extending inner-party democracy, the ever broader democratisation of social life in the spheres of economics and politics, and the drawing of ever broader masses of people into direct participation in deciding public questions. This practical side, which consists of expanding individual rights and freedoms and of teaching people how to use their ever greater political freedom, is of immense social significance. This is certainly what Lenin had in mind when he said that under socialism every cook should become a leader of the state.

There is no doubt that the socialist system has accomplished much in this field of the political activisation of the masses and preparing them for a vigorous political role in the state administration. This is shown by the actual development of social and political life in the socialist countries—though we often fail to make known what has already been accomplished in this respect. But it is also necessary clearly to recognise the difficulties involved. These arise primarily from the conservatism of social institutions, even those created by the revolution. People simply get used to certain methods of administration.

Experience teaches, and often in dramatic fashion, that we are rather inclined to delay the process of democratisation than to hasten it. This is because those in leading positions feel their responsibility for the outcome of the struggles taking place, and adopt an attitude of cautious deliberation towards important decisions. That is correct and understandable. But it must be remembered that if too much liberalism is a mistake for which we may pay dearly, the price of checking the process of democratisation of social life is equally heavy. This is why, with full deliberation and caution, it is necessary to create conditions for continuous democratisation.

Of key importance in our situation is the development of democracy within the Party. Owing to the particular role of the working class in guiding our entire social life, the working class party is the best school for social leadership and its condition is at the same time the index of democracy. It is no accident that this became a central question for us in Poland in 1955—56. It now presents itself differently, but continues to occupy the centre of attention. It is a matter of enormous importance to increase the activity of the party membership in assuming initiative and undertaking decisions, to enlarge the element of democracy in democratic centralism, to strengthen the organisation and launch effective struggle against all expressions of bureaucracy and tendencies to separate the state apparatus from the masses. It is also of great importance to respect the right of party members to maintain and defend their opinions within the provisions of the party rules—a right so strongly defended by Lenin. But this is a difficult and delicate matter, especially since this right was *de facto* abolished for many years in Poland. It is difficult to get rid of the results of many years of contrary practice. It is easier to condemn in words the distortions of the period of the personality cult than to change the practices which were then dominant. The cause of the trouble is not only rigidity and being sunk in routine—it is also the fear of making serious mistakes. But worst of all is the dread of difficulties: for to change prevailing practices means to create a new situation and to create new difficulties. Of course, to do this requires deliberation and hasty action would be harmful. But the need for a change cannot be doubted.

The propagation of socialist humanism within the party and in society at large is a vital matter, precisely because of the hesitations and resistances I have mentioned. For resistance and hesitation do not for the most part stem from ill will, but from limited perspectives and misunderstanding the situation. No one can lay down a general rule for evaluating actual situations. It is possible only to provide a better orientation. Every member of our society, every party member, and above all everyone who holds any responsible post, should have a full understanding of the humanist goals of socialism. Limitations on freedom should be recognised for what they are, and it should be understood that they are to be eliminated as soon as possible. The desire to do away with all such limitations, and not to perpetuate them in the name of some higher authority, helps to solve immediate tasks.

Creative discussion and working out of ideas was to some extent frowned on in our country of recent years.

That was certainly wrong; and there would not have been such energetic ideological discussions among us later on, if they had not been of social significance. We want more not less discussion in the schools and universities, through all the media of mass communication, through lectures, and so on. Every detail of such activity is important.

Among the most serious problems of individual freedom are those of freedom of conscience and of speech, that is, freedom to think and speak according to one's convictions. Here I propose to deal with only one aspect of this problem, the freedom to entertain and express various views in the fields of science and·art.

A humanist defends freedom in all its aspects. But as distinct from at least some of the varieties of bourgeois humanism, a Marxist is always conscious that questions of freedom are social questions; the socialist humanist, therefore, considers every question of freedom in its social and political implications, and not in the abstract.

Freedom of discussion, the free clash of opposing views, undoubtedly provides the best conditions for the development of science and of culture generally. If political authorities attempt to settle controversial problems in this field by toplevel decisions, that can only do harm. For it is always a matter of the progress of thought, and so of the discovery of new and previously unknown truth which may often displace what was accepted before. Unless we are prophets or clairvoyants we can never know in advance what new truth will be, and the only road to its discovery is that of free research and discussion. Marxism regards knowledge as an always unfinished process, no part of which is immutable or complete in itself. It is surprising, therefore, that we sometimes find the contrary practice among Marxists.

We must also reckon here with the intrinsic conservatism of most people in matters of artistic taste and also in relation to certain scientific conceptions. Innovators in art, and sometimes in science too, win recognition only many years after their deaths. As the proverb says, noone is a prophet in his own country; it might be added, that noone is a prophet in his own lifetime. Perhaps that is not so bad, for it is worse when someone hailed as a prophet in his lifetime is erased from the pages of history by posterity. As a rule, geniuses have been neglected or persecuted, derided and belittled. This is why when we take a dislike to anything new in scientific or artistic creation, when we are inclined to condemn it offhand, we should in due modesty recall Bach and Beethoven, Van Gogh and Modigliani, and many, many others. Perhaps we are witnessing the birth of a new Copernicus, or a new Boyle? The demand for creative freedom in science and art would be not only obvious but banal if it were not for its political repercussions. At least some fields of science and art are directly related to politics; they are expressions of progressive or retrogressive social tendencies, and may have a progressive or reactionary effect on society. Only a utopian can ignore this fact and demand absolute freedom of creation. Nor can we treat as absolute the right of scientists and artists themselves to solve scientific and artistic questions, as the only people competent to judge such matters. Their competence and authority are not always complete.

There can be no doubt that only specialists can resolve theoretical controversies in mathematics and physics— current controversies about quantum mechanics, for example. Noone else should interfere in such controversies, unless he wishes to hinder scientific progress.

But the case is different if the controversy has to do with the principles of economic planning, the character of the state, of the class structure of society. Here there is no clear division between science and politics, or between scholars and practical workers. For these are problems which practical workers understand in general very well, and often much better than representative of the academic world. The subject matter of such problems is indissolubly connected with politics, both in the sense that it is shaped under the influence of given political ideas and that the problems themselves influence politics.

It is obvious that a controversy about atonality is a purely musical one. Only a very imprudent person would dare to interfere from outside in such a controversy; he would gain nothing but ridicule for his pains. But it is another matter with the ideological content of a novel or poem, which is closely connected with politics regardless of its artistic merits. It is shaped under the influence of politics and reacts on politics.

I have deliberately considered extreme examples, between which could be blended a whole palette of intermediate colours. My aim was only to illustrate the fact that there is no room here for absolute standards, and that everything has to be assessed and broken down in relation to concrete circumstances.

Yet, proceeding from the principles of socialist humanism and its conception of the development of the human personality, it is possible to reach conclusions of great practical importance on such intricate questions. One such conclusion is that political intervention in matters of artistic and scientific creation should be exceptional and limited to areas of clear political implication. Of course, a certain element of subjectivism in choice and evaluation is involved here, and there is no escape from it. Scientific and artistic creation do become entangled with politics, and typical situations of conflict consequently arise.

But political intervention here should be indirect. What is wanted is to indicate to cultural workers and scientists the social needs which their work may satisfy— for example, by suggesting themes of particular social importance; and to influence them ideologically, by helping to shape their world outlook, especially in relation to the scientific understanding of society. This constitutes the most essential content of party guidance of science and art, apart from the organisational side of their development, which belongs to the area of politics but cannot be put on the same plane as freedom of creative thought.

Again, when we speak of science and art, and of the development of human personality on connection with freedom of thought and speech, it is necessary to have in mind not only the existing situation but also the future. The goal of communism is full and unhindered freedom, while limitations on freedom are temporary and induced by unfortunate political necessity.

Do the above considerations about freedom of discussion and differences of opinion apply within the party? The question is rhetorical, and none but a positive answer can be expected. For it is obvious that the science of Marxism is subject to the same general laws of development as other sciences, and, like them, can develop only through free discussion. The answer is not, however, so self-evident as would appear at first sight. It is not so self-evident, because a false understanding of party discipline and of its application in such specific areas as science and the arts can lead to deplorable results, as we know now by sad experience.

Yet apart from distorted vision resulting from over-zealousness, the question is entirely clear, in my opinion, and it is not necessary to add much to what has already been said. It may perhaps be stated that a party author should always be conscious of his special ideological responsibility and never act on impulse, particularly in political affairs. He should always remember that he is also a political leader and is morally and politically responsible for what he writes. This does not, however, contradict the principle that scientists or artists who base themselves on Marxism can develop their science and art only under conditions of free research and discussion, only when the field is open for a clash of opinions. Of course, this creates its own difficulties and political dangers, but the progress of science and art is impeded unless such risks are taken. Such impediments must in turn react upon the political line, if only by weakening the possibilities for correcting errors committed in political practice.

In his letter to Bebel of May 2nd, 1891, Freidrich Engels, co-founder of scientific socialism, expressed himself in no uncertain terms in relation to a controversy which had blown up among the leaders of German social-democracy.

"For you—for the party—socialist science is necessary," he wrote, "but it cannot exist without freedom of motion. So it is necessary to put up with a certain amoung of unpleasantness, and is better to accept it with a certain dignity, without bristling up. Even a petty misunderstanding—not to speak of a conflict— between the German party and German socialist science would be a very serious misfortune. It is understood that the administration and you personally do and must have a great influence over *Neue Zeit* and all other publications. *Vorwarts* always boasts of the inviolability of free discussion, but one does not see much of it. You cannot imagine how strange the desire to apply compulsion appears here, abroad, where people are accustomed to the oldest leaders bearing responsibility for their parties... Besides, you must not forget that discipline in a large party can absolutely never be as harsh as in some small section."

Of course, this statement refers to different conditions from our's. Concrete social needs and political necessities must always affect the manner in which creative workers avail themselves of freedom. Nevertheless, Engels' statement retains its value for us.

14

THE QUEST FOR HAPPINESS[i]

What is happiness? This problem is easy to solve emotionally, but hard to analyse. To write scientifically about it is not only difficult but risky, and the first thing to do is to define a point of departure.

Two approaches may be made: (1) the positive approach, which seeks to distinguish the components of the individual's subjective state of happiness and to define the sum of wellbeing the possession of which equals happiness; (2) the negative approach, which seeks to discover what things prevent the individual from being happy and how they can be overcome. These approaches, though related, are very different. For it is one thing to state necessary conditions, and another to state sufficient conditions. Removal of obstacles which obstruct the individual's happiness is a necessary but not a sufficient condition for happiness; it will not necessarily make him happy, since that must depend on other conditions which are connected with the individuality of the particular person—his own physical and mental state, and the way he has been brought up and conditioned by society. This is why the cause of one individual's happiness may be a source of unhappiness to others, when we consider the variability of people's requirements

This chapter is based on the author's contribution to the sixteenth international conference on philosophy, Geneva, September 1961.

and dispositions as well as changes in social conditions.

In a positive approach to the problem, it is useless to try to make a list of concrete factors assuring people's happiness. When we speak of the state of a happy individual we are speaking of his feelings; and even if we try to lend this question a pseudo-objective character by referring to the condition of wellbeing the possession of which constitutes happiness, we still find ourselves in areas so highly saturated with subjectivity that every attempt to find a universally valid answer is doomed to failure. It is not merely a paradox that some people must be unhappy in order to feel happy. The ways of the individual psyche are far too complicated to be encompassed in any formula.

The negative approach considers conditions necessary to happiness, that is to say, obstacles the removal of which is necessary. This approach cannot answer the question "What is happiness?" nor its transposition "When is a person happy?" Nevertheless, the analysis of conditions necessary for happiness is, in my opinion, more interesting and fruitful, particularly from the social point of view, than the seemingly broader and more positive approach of examining the conditions sufficient for happiness.

I do not wish to imply by this that the latter approach is not worth while. If we bear always in mind the dose of subjectivity it contains and guard against consequent mystification, an investigation of the conditions sufficient for happiness may add something to our knowledge of human individuality and demonstrate the futility of seeking a formula for "complete happiness" for everyone. A negative answer is also an answer, and a demonstration of the futility of searching is also a discovery. But while the positive approach to the question of happiness yields primarily negative results, the narrower, seemingly negative approach, that of investigating the necessary conditions for happiness, yields mainly positive results.

It leads to positive conclusions about what is to be done by way of social action in the quest for happiness.

I have in mind, concretely, the investigation of the social conditions required for human happiness.

Everyone is happy or unhappy in his own way. Yet despite the subjectivity of the feelings of happiness and unhappiness, and despite the variability of individuals, all people have something in common. None is happy when deprived of something he needs in some phase of his life, and there are things which all people need. Except for pathological cases, to be deprived of these things makes everyone unhappy. This fact unites the outlooks and feelings of all people, without in any way contradicting their individual eccentricities. We are thus able to grasp something stable and definite in the general haze of the problem, something which readily lends itself to definition and may become the subject of social action.

A person suffering hunger and want, who cannot satisfy his basic minimum needs as determined by the historical stage of development of society, is not and cannot be happy. There is a well known Chinese fable about a king who was seeking the shirt of a happy man; when he finally found such a man, it turned out that he had no shirt. Although of respectable antiquity, this fable is profoundly false and was clearly invented by people who did possess shirts. It was addressed to those without, to discourage them from demanding shirts. Hunger and want certainly do not make people happy. On the contrary, as the causes of real and deep unhappiness they goad people to anger and revolt. Such revolt is a struggle for the right to happiness, for the removal of whatever stands in the way of happiness, although the abolition of hunger and want does not of itself make people happy.

But hunger and want are not the only widespread social causes of unhappiness. Such are also the lack of freedom, national oppression, economic exploitation, racial persecution, and all other expressions of social inequality. In all such cases people are deprived of what they need. And though to be deprived of freedom or social equality is not the same as to be denied the material means of life, men feel their lack no less strongly and painfully. The deprivation of freedom is as strong an incentive to revolt as are hunger and want. This too is a struggle for personal happiness, a struggle for a condition which is not sufficient of itself to bring happiness but the lack of which brings unhappiness.

Obviously, there are other deprivations which also make the individual unhappy. For instance, unrequited love, or unsatisfied ambition. These are so common that they can be regarded as typical social phenomena. But there is a basic difference between such deprivations and those which we have considered above. Here are two categories of deprivation, in the first of which it is a matter of obstacles to the individual's happiness created by existing social relations, and in the second a matter of obstacles created by the individual's own psychological makeup or by his relations to other individuals—as in the case of disappointment in love. Hence social intervention is possible to remove deprivations of the first category, since by changing the social relations the source of the individual's unhappiness can be eliminated. But society cannot intervene to remove deprivations of the second sort. At any rate, it cannot intervene directly: social action can have an indirect effect, by changing the social conditions which shape the individual's personality, though such an effect is generally produced unconsciously, spontaneously.

The first sort of deprivations have for centuries figured in the programmes of progressive social movements, the essence of which, under different titles and names, has been the struggle to create more favourable conditions for people's happiness—or, to put it in another way, to create more favourable conditions for the development of the human personality. In this sense, those who see the realisation of conditions necessary for the individual's happiness as the goal of their social activity are, in the best sense of the word, humanists. And this consideration provides us with criteria for assessing social movements and their programmes, as well as different varieties of humanism.

All social movements speak of the people's happiness and include the struggle for it in their programmes. For who would support them otherwise? Even anti-humanist ideologies of genocide and hate, like Hitlerism, as well as every variety of colonialism and racism, make use of phrases about fighting for human happiness. In their case, we may ask for whose happiness are the fascist "supermen" and the racists fighting? It seems to depend on whom they consider to be a human being. The modern anti-humanists have no few precursors in this respect, beginning with some of the humanists of antiquity, who considered slaves to be talking chattels. This demonstrates, incidentally, the historically relative character of different varieties of humanism.

Scientific socialism is essentially humanist, and the essence of its humanism is its conception of the happiness of the individual. Everything in Marxism—its philosophy, political economy and political theory—is subordinated to this. For Marxism is the sum of theoretical instruments which serve one practical aim, the struggle for a happier human life. This is how Marx understood the question while still young, when he said that a revolutionary philosophy is the ideological weapon of the proletariat. Such is the meaning of the Marxist postulate of the unity of theory and practice. And this is why the theory of happiness takes on a specific form with Marxism—not as the abstract reflection of the meaning of happiness or of its subjective components, but as the revolutionary idea of that transformation of social relations which would make possible the creation of the conditions for a happy life by removing the social obstacles to such a life. Marxist socialism approaches the problem of individual happiness from its negative side, that is to say, it investigates the social obstacles to human happiness and how they can be removed. It is this approach which brings positive results, because of its realism.

In many countries people go hungry and live in misery. Two thirds of the world's population suffer permanent hunger. It is Marxist socialism which shows the road of social change which can abolish this state of affairs and create better conditions for human life. Here is no preaching, no moralising by well-off people. The hungry hear in the ideas of Marxism the answer to their yearning for happiness, and feel in them the full depth of the humanism so beautifully expressed by Marx's friend, Heinrich Heine, in his *Winter's Tale*:

> A new song and a better one—
> Friend, shall I bring that song to birth?
> The Kingdom of Heaven that is promised,
> We want to build upon the earth.
>
> We want on earth a happy life
> And not a life of dark despair.
> Let not the lazy belly squander
> What hands produce with diligent care.
>
> Here in abundance bread is growing,
> Enough for all, if so we please;
> Enough of myrtles and roses, laughter
> And beauty—and, as well, sweet peas.
>
> Sweet peas indeed for everyone
> As soon as the pods burst and spill.
> The heavens we'll leave aloft, reserved
> Only for angels and sparrows still.

Marxist socialism has the same approach to the problems of national oppression, religious or racial persecution, subjection of women, economic exploitation—it shows people the way to free themselves from unhappy conditions. Marxism not only teaches that life could be happy, but it shows how to make it so; it organises and mobilises the people against everything that denies them happiness. We do not offer happiness in the afterlife, but struggle for it in this life with confidence of success. Marxism is a political theory which embraces humanism, morality, happiness. Is it strange, then, that it appeals to those who suffer and yearn for a better, happier life? Is it surprising that its call is heard everywhere on earth by those to whom were addressed the words of the *International*: "Arise, ye prisoners of starvation..."?

Our theory of happiness is a theory of the social conditions necessary for happiness. Whether under such conditions each and every individual will enjoy complete happiness depends on the individual. It is not possible to guarantee happiness to everyone—to serve it to them on a plate, so to speak; but it *is* possible to create suitable conditions for the happiness of all. Marxist socialism concentrates its attention on creating such conditions for happiness.

Some authors tell us that the age of ideologies has now come to an end. As the word "ideology" has about twenty different meanings, it is difficult to know quite what they mean. If, however, they understand the word in the sense in which it occurs in such phrases as "feudal ideology", "bourgeois ideology" and "socialist ideology", that is, as the system of ideas and attitudes to social life current in specific historical conditions, then they are certainly mistaken. Not only has the age of ideologies not come to an end, but ideology now plays a more active role in social development than ever before. It plays an ever more powerful and efficacious part in the struggle between the two competing systems of capitalism and socialism.

The coexistence of these two social-economic systems is a fact. It does not follow that if this coexistence is peaceful all conflicting interests and disputes between socialist and capitalist states disappear, and competition between them ceases. This competition cannot cease so long as two different social-economic formations remain, for it could cease only with the downfall or collapse of one or other of the systems.

Two systems, two ideologies: the ideological differences involved are differences in viewpoint on the ideals of social life, on the proper structure of society and the way of running it. We may leave aside here the question of the origin and social source of the differences which distinguish a Marxist from a Tomist, an Existentialist or an adherent of any other non-Marxist philosophy. But Tomists, Existentialists, Marxists and all, if they are to retain their common sense in matters of philosophy, must agree that the advocates of private property in means of production and those who advocate the social ownership of the means of production entertain different values and different ideas of the proper way of running a modern society. And this is precisely a difference of ideology.

This is why the objections of some Western politicians to a peaceful coexistence in which ideological differences are continued is either extremely disingenuous or extremely naive.

The central question of international relations today is not that of removing ideological differences, which cannot be done, but of removing the danger of an armed conflict which would bring catastrophe to the whole human race. With peaceful coexistence, when the danger of armed conflict recedes, ideological differences remain and will, in fact, become the centre of attention. Ideology will play an ever greater role in the competition between the two systems in the measure that the danger of armed conflict recedes. This is not only unavoidable, but right and proper. Both competing camps, or at any rate the parties or groups directing them, are, presumably, convinced of the superiority of their own way of life. Since people cannot be compelled by armed force to accept either system—and that is a very good thing for the people—they must be convinced of the superiority of one or other system. Peaceful coexistence does not mean a stabilised world divided into spheres of influence in the old diplomatic tradition. Even if the side with "the preponderance of strength" desired such a division, life would annul it. So long as armed force does not intervene, people will choose whatever in their opinion is the best way of life, and they will do so regardless of any government's or party's wishes. Peaceful coexistence does not guarantee the *status quo*, the unalterability of the established social orders. The accumulation of ideological differences means a sharpened competitive struggle for the minds and hearts of the people. And to what must the protagonists of the two systems and two ideologies appeal in order to win the assent of the people? To facts, which on the principle that "words speak but examples move" are the strongest arguments. This brings us back to our main theme, the social conditions necessary for the happiness of the individual.

In the final count, the ideological differences of which we have been speaking, the differences in people's views and attitudes to social life, come down to the divergence of views on the social conditions required for individual happiness and on the methods of their realisation. Let us consider the disputes over the principle of private or public ownership of the means of production, or over the question of an internationalist or nationalist standpoint on the relations between nations and states. Regardless of how they are argued, these disputes are disputes about how to live better, about what conditions assure to people the best opportunities for a happy life. The theory of happiness once again descends from the heights of abstraction to the firm ground of social life.

Under conditions of peaceful coexistence the competitive struggle will more and more be waged in the realm of ideology, by presenting to people various views of a happy life. As a result, this struggle will assume the ever clearer form of a clash between different variants of humanism. I said above that even barbarous anti-humanism tries to speak to the people in the language of a theory of happiness. This is certainly a sign of the times. But the clash between different types of genuine humanism is the crucial issue.

The contemporary humanisms are of different origin and of varying nature, both in their content and in their social background. Apart from the general slogan of the full flowering of the human personality as the goal of all variants of humanism, there is a vast difference between them. Compare, for example, the materialism and militancy of socialist humanism with the creationist, contemplative humanism of Christianity, or the subjectivist humanism of Existentialism. The different social and philosophical points of departure of different humanisms determine the way they approach the problem of human happiness, and whether their outlook is optimistic or pessimistic, militant or contemplative and moralising.

But for the people who already possess conditions for a happier life, the practical question of how to defend and develop those social achievements is of far greater importance than the philosophical discussion of the reasons for existence and the world views of conflicting humanisms. For such people, subtle philosophical disputes about the autonomous or socially conditioned character of the individual have no significance, or almost none.

From this point of view two questions are especially important. Are there any soundly based methods for the people's liberation from social evil? And are there any examples of such methods having been applied in practice, to convince those who have doubts? Socialist humanism knows such methods, as well as practical evidence for their efficacity; and this constitutes its strength, and the secret of its success. Whoever does not want to understand this, and prefers to indulge in wishful thinking and to deny reality, will certainly be overwhelmed by the progress of real life and lose the competitive struggle.

One may object to socialism in its entirety, one may stubbornly deny its humanism, but the hungry and exploited will sooner or later come to understand that hunger will finally cease in this world of potential abundance only when the system of exploitation is abolished. No hope of rewards in the hereafter, no consolations of absolute morality, will stand up in face of the simple fact that it is possible so to arrange social life that people will not have to work for others and go hungry.

The situation is the same with regard to national and racial oppression. What enthuses fighters against enslavement are the real perspectives of liberation and the attractiveness of its examples. For the peoples of Asia, Africa and Latin America the teachers and models will continue to be the Soviet Union and People's China, and certainly not Portugal, Belgium, Great Britain or the United States of America, which are themselves colonialists or patrons of the colonialists. Words are of no avail when facts speak so loudly. And in this respect too, socialist humanism has a great advantage over its competitors.

Finally, the question of peace is the great subject of any people's plebiscite on different conceptions of humanism. There is no more important question for people who are fighting for personal happiness. And here, too, it is primarily a matter of deeds and not of words. The question stands: for or against total disarmament, the only rational way out of the difficult situation humanity faces today. There can be no doubt that the decisions and deeds on this question will turn the scales in the choice between different varieties of humanism.

We live in the beautiful epoch when the problem of the happiness of the individual and the conditions for its fulfillment has advanced from the realm of words and philosophical speculation to that of concrete struggle and practical realisation. This fact must gladden the heart of every true humanist. It is becoming more and more difficult to remain a bystander. It is becoming harder and harder to remain only a platonic advocate of good causes and shun the struggle for them. Life compels a choice, and one must therefore decide. This fact puts its stamp on the struggle between various conceptions of humanism. Independent of conscious choice, under the pressure of the needs of life and the longing for happiness, the words of the good poet are being translated into all languages:

"We want on earth a happy life."